To Si

the Server

at Wimbleda
2013 !

Regards,

Space

the Server

by Spencer Vignes

The Server

Pitch Publishing
10 Beresford Court
Sommerhill Road
Hove, East Sussex
BN3 1RH

Email: info@pitchpublishing.co.uk
www.pitchpublishing.co.uk

First published 2003.

A catalogue record for this book is available
from the British Library.

ISBN: 0-9542460-2-0

Cover design by Paul Camillin.

Page design and layout by Jigsaw Design,
Worthing, West Sussex.

Printed and bound in Great Britain by
Cox and Wyman Ltd.

In Memory of Geoff Vignes, 1944–1993
Hope this makes up for the Mercedes

Contents

Acknowledgements

First, my wife Alex, who not only encouraged me to write this book but also proofread the original manuscript. A big thank you to everyone who fed, watered, housed and played me during my journey, and to my father, mother and Jimmy Connors for introducing me to the game of tennis in the first place.

Cheers to Madness, The Pretenders and XTC for helping to keep me sane with their music during the writing process, to the Grade Twos – Vincent, Barry, Steve, Gary and Kevin – for the send-off, and all at Pitch Publishing for their faith and support.

Prologue

It all began something like this.

The year was 1984. The place, a sixties-style secondary school maths classroom in a town in southern England. Sat around a large, graffiti-covered table, nine boys in their early teens were discussing the previous night's television. On the agenda was:

a) the children's TV show *Animal Magic*, featuring an attack on the ageing presenter Johnny Morris by an electric eel

b) an appearance on *Top Of The Pops* by a weird-looking girl in a pink wig warbling about being touched for the very first time, and

c) an odd film called *The Swimmer* starring Burt Lancaster spending a day ploughing through the pools of his wealthy friends and neighbours in suburban Connecticut.

Now my old wine-stained movie guide uses various words to describe *The Swimmer*. They include 'memorable' and 'unsettling'... but 'bollocks' appeared to be the main one doing the rounds among 5Z2 that Friday morning. Hardly surprising really. The plot does, after all, revolve around an

1

advertising executive on the verge of a nervous breakdown going for a 91-minute dip. Not exactly cutting-edge stuff for the average adolescent, particularly in a year of *The Terminator* and *Ghostbusters* at the movies.

However, one of the boys – okay, I'll cut the crap, me – was busy fighting *The Swimmer*'s corner. I'd liked it. It was refreshing, a pleasant alternative to the monotonous crash-bang-wallop film-making style of the time. I'd also recently seen Burt star alongside Deborah Kerr in *From Here To Eternity*, and frankly, anyone who got to snog girls while rolling round in the Pacific surf was going to get this sexually frustrated youth's vote every time.

But there was something else. *The Swimmer* had given me an idea, one that might take care of a spare few hours one weekend in the Sussex village where I lived. Modelling myself on muscle-bound Burt, I was going to play tennis through the back gardens of every house in Warnham with a court – all three of them. It was my favourite sport at the time and if planned right, it would give me a genuine reason for walking past the home of Kim Marlow – long blonde hair, eyes of blue, totally out of my league – at least twice. Forget my lanky build and failing eyesight. For one afternoon only, I was going to be *The Server*.

Of course it never came off, in the way that most hare-brained male 'Hey, let's climb Everest this weekend!' schemes don't. Warnham was, still is, a small place. I knew the owners of each court pretty well, and I'm sure they'd have all welcomed me with open arms. On the chosen day something far more important must have cropped up, like banging a football against a wall 946 times. Perhaps Tina Taylor, owner of the finest breasts south of Reigate, simply walked past and erased my memory banks, as she had a habit of doing around that time.

Eighteen years later and pretty much the same group of boys – now sporting regulation beer bellies and grade two haircuts designed to hide the advanced stages of receding – are sitting in a bar a mile or so from their old maths classroom. A mixture of fatherhood, work, relationships and living at opposite ends of the country means we don't get to see too much of each other these days. That means the drinking is heavier and the talking louder than the average Saturday night, as it always tends to be when men get together in large groups for the first time in a while. As though bawling at each other from point blank range somehow makes up for lost time.

After a few jars, the conversation turns from England's chances in the forthcoming football World Cup to life 'up north' in Yorkshire, where I had moved three years earlier with my wife, Alex. I'm saying how everything is fine, work is busy, marriage is great and how wonderful it is that my other half is almost four months pregnant. And then I casually mention that the following day I'm setting off on a bit of a trip, one that won't take me home for a couple of months.

There's a pause, and one of the Grade Twos asks me where I'm going. So I start explaining how I'd seen *The Swimmer* again, and that it had inspired me to revive an idea I'd had when we were kids, only now on a grander scale. Armed with my trusty Donnay racket and a bag of balls, I was going to play tennis on every court I happened to come across on a journey from my childhood home of Warnham to my adult one in the West Yorkshire town of Normanton, some 250 miles away. I'd be doing the trip along England's back roads in my 1969 Morris Minor, the same make of car as my late father had used to ferry me to tennis tournaments as a child. I wouldn't be following any particular route, just going where the wind – and the Morris – took me. And each time I spotted a tennis court, I had to stop and challenge the first person I saw to have a hit with me, whether it be Boris Becker or blind old Mrs Brady on her way back from bingo.

Another pause, only this time a tad longer.

"Well, it's different I suppose," says the first Grade Two eventually. "Anyone up for moving on somewhere else?"

This lot are notoriously hard to impress, and there's no sign of the ecstatic reception my idea had initially been given by some media-type friends I'd used as sounding boards. They down their dregs faster than a Greg Rusedski first-service and get up to leave. I follow suit. End of conversation.

An hour or so later and the subject of my tennis trip has been revived over a curry. The gang is interested, but I can tell at least two of them are itching to jab a finger in my rib cage and scream, "HOW CAN YOU AFFORD TO JUST FUCK OFF AND PLAY TENNIS FOR WEEKS?!" And I know exactly where they're coming from. I went through a stage of being unable to pick up a travel book without thinking along the same lines. Sod the poor state of the Australian rail network between Koolyanobbing and Tarcoola. By page three, I'd be too busy trying to fathom out how anyone can spend five years teaching kangaroos the lyrics to Shakin' Stevens records, while continuing to pay the bills on a four-bedroomed house in Clapham. And who's feeding the cat while they're gone?

First Grade Two: "Well, it beats working for a living, I'll give you that."

Me: "Look. I've worked bloody hard over the last few months to be able to take time off to do this. God knows whether it'll come off, but it's something I really want to have a go at."

Second Grade Two: "And Alex is fine with you doing this?"

Me: "Yep. We've always said that if there's anything one of us really wants to do in life, any big ambition, then the other one will help them 100 per cent to do it."

First Grade Two: "And that also goes for when one of you happens to be pregnant?"

Me: "Um, yeah. Anyway, they say the first three months of any pregnancy are the most critical, and she's safely past that now. And it's not as though I'll be on the other side of the world. Heaven forbid anything should happen, I'm only a phone call and a couple of hours drive away."

Third Grade Two: "A couple of hours drive away – in a Morris Minor?"

Me: "All right, four or five. But it's a good little car. She'll get me home just fine in an emergency."

First Grade Two: "Okay. So you're going in search of tennis courts. What happens if you find one, you pull over, and there's nobody around to play?"

Me: "Then I wait for 20 minutes. If nobody shows up, then I'll serve one ball and carry on to the next court. And so on."

Third Grade Two (with a hint of smugness): "What about if you see one in someone's back garden. What you gonna do then?"

Me: "Then I walk up the path, ring the doorbell and ask if they'll come and have a knock with me."

Everyone laughs. They are my oldest friends and for some reason, even after all these years, their opinions still matter to me. Then again they're also the kind of guys you want to keep on the right side of. They remember the time I paid good money for an LP by the Pointer Sisters. And if they get their way, they'll make sure *I'll* always remember it too.

The bill arrives and we prepare to go our separate ways for another year. It's been a good evening and I've got a warm feeling inside me, one that isn't simply down to the eight pints of bitter and chicken vindaloo I've managed to put away. It's the kind you get from meeting up with old friends and realising that despite divorce, redundancy, bereavement and any amount of shit that life throws at you, some things really don't change. Deep down, we're all still a bunch of Muppets.

"Good luck, Goran," bawls the third Grade Two as he stumbles off towards the taxi rank. "Give my love to Anna Kournikova when you see her."

CHAPTER ONE

Going Back

**"I'm swimming home. I've figured it out.
There's a river of pools all the way to
my house."**
Burt Lancaster as Ned Merrill, *The Swimmer*

Tennis courts.

They're out there. Almost 40,000 of them at the last count, all across Britain. Okay, so a large percentage don't have nets, look like they've staged a small civil war, and tend to be used more during the winter for drug deals than tennis. But they're there. In public parks, back gardens, on council estates, at private clubs and, in at least two cities that I can think of, in the middle of traffic round-abouts. Hundreds of square miles of tarmac, grass and Astroturf just burning to be enjoyed during the 50 weeks of the year when Wimbledon isn't on TV.

I first discovered them in 1978 at the age of nine, my very own year zero with tennis and life. That was when my parents upped sticks and moved us from the claustrophobia of London's south west suburbs to the village of Warnham.

Warnham was the kind of place that made Laurie Lee's *Cider With Rosie* look like something out of *Blade Runner*. It was a world where the sun always shone, work was easy to find, and everyone came out of their houses every hour on the hour to dance in the streets to *One Step Beyond* by Madness. Kids scrumped apples from dawn to dusk, then went snogging in the churchyard until bedtime. Anyone suspected of being a property developer was hung in public on the village green after Sunday lunch.

Graham Greene, who helped put Sussex on the global map with his novel *Brighton Rock*, once said that 'an unhappy childhood is a writer's goldmine.' So I'm going to give you a few early words of warning. If you are currently reading this in a bookshop and subscribe to Graham's theory, then you're probably better off buying that book about Shakey-crooning kangaroos. Because my childhood was a complete gas. And I loved where I grew up.

Shortly after we moved to Sussex my parents bought me my first tennis racket. A metal one just like my hero Jimmy Connors used. I'd spend hours out practising, expelling loud grunts and telling imaginary umpires to get stuffed, just like Jimmy did. Warnham didn't have any public tennis courts but, being the kind of communally spirited place it was, there was usually someone around willing to lend you a private one. I would alternate between the slightly battered court at the Vicarage (where you stood the chance of being brought squash and biscuits by the vicar's wife) and the one on Knob Hill owned by the Hodgson family (better condition, but no snacks). Swearing was a straight-to-hell offence at the Vicarage so the older I got – and the more colourful my insults to the imaginary umpire became – the more I started using the Hodgson's, until it became my very own Centre Court.

I was never anything other than an average player. I entered numerous tournaments and would have competed for my secondary school, only the two courts on the upper playground doubled as a car park, making play possible for about thirty seconds a year. I went for lessons in the nearby market town of Horsham, and used to go home baffled as to why the coaches always ignored me in favour of the rich kids who arrived in Mercedes. I took part in a county coaching-squad session, where I was made to feel about as welcome as Mark Chapman at a John Lennon Convention. Oh yeah, and I won the 1985 Warnham Youth Club Cup in front of four people, two of whom weren't my parents.

Soon afterwards I finally discovered sex, pubs and London, where I ended up moving to go to college. My parents left Warnham and moved to Wales. And somewhere along the line I put down

11

my tennis racket, stopped playing and fell out of love with the game.

That was until 2001, when a surreal sequence of events led to me rediscovering my passion for the sport. The year began with an over-zealous centre-forward shattering several bones in my right hand during a football match, including all the bones in my little finger. Lying in a hospital bed recovering from plastic surgery, one thing bothered me more than anything else. It wasn't where the next pay cheque would be coming from, something you'd think might be high on the priority list for a right-handed freelance writer. It was whether I'd ever be able to hold a tennis racket again, strange considering that the last time I'd hit a ball in anger, Spandau Ballet were still having hits.

The urge to play again gave me something to focus on throughout the eight months of intensive physio that followed, during which the 'surreal sequence' continued with the wonderfully eccentric Goran Ivanisevic winning Wimbledon in the most dramatic final since Tim Henman was at junior school. It reminded me of Warnham, of watching Borg, McEnroe and Connors on the tiny TV screen in our living room – an era when every final seemed to be a classic. Listening to the Croatian clinch the title on the car radio while driving home across the Pennines from Manchester, I couldn't help but feel that I'd been missing out on something over the past 16 years.

The sequence was completed one evening that summer when I sat down to watch television and *The Swimmer* came on. It was the first time I'd seen Burt doing his front crawl since that night in 1984, right after Madonna had reduced the ranks of 5Z2 to gibbering wrecks with her *Top Of The Pops* performance. Everything came flooding back. No, not the effect Maddy had had on my adolescent mess of a body, but the half-baked plot to play tennis through the back gardens of Warnham.

My writer's brain, the one that permanently scans life on the lookout for interesting yarns, went into overdrive. Why not go back to Warnham and see if the courts were still there? If they were, then perhaps I could serve a ball or two on them, maybe even play a game against someone. And now that I wasn't 14 anymore, and was free to stay out as long as I wanted after 9pm, why not just keep on playing? Right out of Sussex, north through England and all the way home to Normanton.

It really was as simple as that, a true eureka moment. A severe workload plus lack of funds would prevent me from setting off during what remained of that summer. But come the following spring, once the weather had improved, I'd be on my way. It sounded like a first-class excuse to visit some interesting places, no doubt meet a few characters, and get my game up to scratch following years of neglect and the football injury. I'd read that almost four million people played tennis on a regular basis in Britain, so it would also give me the perfect opportunity to find out exactly who they were.

I have to confess that another slightly more devious, ulterior motive for my trip emerged before I got round to wiping the dust from my racket and juicing up the Morris Minor ready for the road. I wanted to see if tennis was still as stuffy and class-conscious as I remembered it, a sport riddled with retired wing commanders and comfortably-off coaches who would rather lock your average teenager in a cage with a Bengal tiger than set them free on a tennis court. How I hoped it had changed, that I'd discover budding Andre Agassis with baseball caps yanked back-to-front being coached on the council courts of Haringey and Handsworth, but I wasn't exactly holding my breath.

Everything went just peachy on the preparation front until, about a week before I'd planned to leave Yorkshire for Sussex, I began to develop a peculiar case of pre-match nerves. At first I thought it might be connected with leaving Alex on her own, especially with her being four months pregnant. But as D-day grew closer, and the nerves continued to grow, the penny finally dropped. I was worried about going back to Warnham.

I'm probably not the first person to feel slightly anxious about returning to the 'home' of their childhood many years after they were last there. Although I still have several close friends in Sussex,

I hadn't been back to little Warnham since my parents left for Cardiff in the late 1980s. People there don't know me as a reasonably successful journalist who got to travel the world and marry a lovely, talented woman. I'm just Spencer Vignes, unnaturally tall 14-year-old with an unhealthy passion for tennis and trains. And a complete chocolate-fireguard when it comes to girls.

As a way of gearing up for what lay in store, I logged onto the internet at home one evening and entered 'Warnham' on a search engine. The results were incredible. My old Scout troop had closed down and Latin American dancing at some fancy studio appeared to have replaced the hourly knees-up sessions to *One Step Beyond*, but very little else seemed to have changed. The pubs, the Comrades Social Club and my junior school (complete with website pictures of my old classroom) were all still there. Colin Funnell, the right-back in my under-13s Saturday morning football team, was now right-back in the amateur village side. The annual Flower Show remained the place to be seen for the over-50s or anyone with a cucumber the length of Brighton's Palace Pier. Mick Hodgson, now a county councillor, still lived in his big house on Knob Hill. And thanks to the online revolution, I had his telephone number.

"So you want to use my court again?" said a familiar voice after I'd explained all about my planned trek.

"Please, providing it's still there."

"Of course it's still there, but you know the one at the Vicarage has been built on?"

This came as a blow. Apparently the church bank account had fallen into bad shape, and the land was sold off. An airline pilot now lived where I'd once hit aces. Or at least tried to. By Mick's reckoning, his was the only court left in the village, the remaining third from my 1984 pipe-dream having been ripped up by some property developer with a taste for public executions long before I'd left for London.

"And the old vicar is dead," he added. "Died last year."

Another blow, especially for the Reverend Francis Doe, who had done as much as anyone to encourage my love of tennis by letting me play at the Vicarage as a nine-year-old.

Mick said his court was mine to use anytime, even if nobody was in.

"You know where it is. Just come round like you always used to. "

I thanked him and replied that I would.

I also scribbled down the number of the only Bed & Breakfast in this picture-postcard village with the sense to advertise on the internet, run by a couple called Chris and Liz Cox. Their names didn't ring any bells at first, not until I'd called and spoken to Chris. It emerged that he'd been on the all-powerful Village Hall Management Committee

(Warnham's answer to the Mafia) with my father, and I'd been at junior school with their daughter, Sophie. Ah yes, I remembered Sophie Cox. But not half as well as I remembered her best friend Alison, the girl I'd shared my first proper kiss with in the churchyard one night after choir practice. And, being a clumsy six-footer with all the romantic charm of Mike Tyson, almost bitten half her right ear off in the process.

We went through all the pleasantries and Chris said how sorry he'd been to hear about my father's death, from bowel cancer, a few years previously.

"So how's your mother?"

"Oh she's fine, just fine, enjoying life in Wales," I replied in a play-it-safe way. Did he know about her lewd obsession with Bryan Ferry, or the assault charge arising from some very unladylike behaviour at a bonfire night party in Lewes?

I made a reservation for that coming Sunday night, and Chris said I could stay in Sophie's room. This threw me a bit until I remembered Sophie wouldn't be in school uniform anymore, and was probably living in Kensington with a husband and 2.4 kids. At 33 years of age, I was finally being given permission to go into a girl's bedroom.

I had a place to stay in Warnham and a venue for my first knock-up. And it wasn't just any court. It was my old Centre Court. Now I had to find someone to play.

CHAPTER TWO

Sophie's Room

"Before, tennis was the main reason I'd get up in the morning. But my past is my past."
Jimmy Connors

These days it has become fashionable to want to trace old school friends, people you haven't seen since Margaret Thatcher was in power and wooden tennis rackets were still cool. Strange, really. Get to know someone really well for five or six years, ignore them for a quarter of the average person's life, then spend ages trying to find them again.

So far I've done my best to resist the 'Friends Reunited' craze on the grounds that those people I have stayed in contact with since my school days – the Grade Twos, for instance – are true mates. Anyone else who fell by the wayside, well, it just wasn't meant to be. Take away lunchtime football kick-abouts or skiving off school to go and see The Cure at Wembley Arena, and what are you

going to have in common with most of them now
anyway?

Only once have I nearly given in to temptation,
and that came soon after I chose Warnham as the
launch pad for my tennis trip. I ditched the idea
after recalling how, in *The Swimmer*, so many of
Burt's long-time friends and neighbours realised
that deep down, they didn't like him. The thought
of people I once regarded as mates telling me what
a wanker I'd been at school, or how many times
they'd got off with Sue Goodwin behind my back
while we were dating, was just too much.

However, I decided to make one big exception.
And that would be Steve Jenkins.

Steve and I spent virtually every summer
weekend during the early eighties playing tennis
against each other. Action-packed, five-set matches
that lasted most of the day until we were dead on
our feet. I always thought of myself as the better
player, the one with all the shots, but Steve had an
uncanny knack of being able to return almost every
ball. He could grind you down. And on court he
had a temper that made John McEnroe look like
Mother Teresa. When Steve hit a wayward volley,
everybody in France, let alone Sussex, got to hear
about it.

I'd hoped that one day some top coach would
catch one of our titanic battles, grab us as we came
off court and say "Gee boys, great match out there.
How about joining me at my world-famous tennis

academy in Florida. All expenses paid. Fame awaits." Of course that was about as likely as the Berlin Wall coming down, a Labour government, or a Canadian wanting to play tennis for Great Britain, but that didn't stop me dreaming.

No doubt about it. My first match back in Warnham, and of my entire journey, had to be against Steve. We'd spoken a couple of times on the phone since our lives went their separate ways around 1986, and once met up at a mutual friend's stag do – though we were both too wrecked to have a sensible conversation. So I told myself that technically, I wouldn't be breaking my strict 'No Friends Reunited' rule if I called and challenged him to a match.

"But I haven't played for years," said Steve after we'd reminisced about our rivalry, and I'd finally got round to throwing down the gauntlet. I told him that made two of us, while I would also be at a disadvantage because of my steadily mending, yet still fragile hand.

"Okay, you're on. But promise me one thing. You'll let me lose my rag at least once, just for old time's sake."

"Glad to. It wouldn't be you if you didn't."

Two days later, I kissed Alex and the beginnings of a bump goodbye and climbed into a 33-year-old Morris Minor, laden with enough rackets, balls, towels and shirts to keep a Davis Cup squad in gear for the next ten years. A little under six hours later and I'd reached the outskirts of Horsham, the little beauty having cantered down England's motorway network smoother than Andre Agassi's balding pate. Exactly how long it would take me to get back home was another matter. Four weeks, six weeks, two months? I hadn't a clue. Only time would tell.

As a former member of the maths room TV discussion panel, and now the proud owner of a cropped haircut, Steve's pre-match preparation that night also ended up involving the Grade Two 2002 Tour of Horsham's pubs and curry houses. Not the wisest of moves by either of us, but at least we'd both be handicapped by double vision for our big clash.

The following morning, I collected Steve and we drove the five or so miles out to the Hodgson family home on the outskirts of Warnham. After several unanswered knocks at the front door, and with no tennis-player-eating Rottweilers in sight, we ambled across the garden to the court and began warming up. The lines were a bit fainter and the surface a touch bumpier than I remembered, but it didn't matter. Like the Warnham I'd read about on the internet, the place had barely changed. I was back on Centre Court, albeit with a hangover, for the first time since the age of 16. And it felt good.

Now don't worry. I'm not going with bore you by describing every stroke of our battle in minute detail (something I'll also be avoiding throughout this book, you'll be glad to hear). Except to say

I won the toss and immediately walloped my first two serves into the net.

"You carry on doing that and this isn't going to be much of a book," mocked my opponent. "You got any more of those or are you gonna make me do some work?"

It soon became obvious that neither Steve nor I were anything like as fit as we'd once been. Here we had a match between two men – one who spends too much time writing about sport to play it, the other just settling into that home cooking, bottle of wine, feet up in front of the telly trap of newly-wedded bliss. Don't get me wrong – we're very happy in our tiny, adult worlds. But there was a time when we'd have sold our grannies just to lace up Ivan Lendl's Nikes. As John McEnroe once said of his rivalry with Bjorn Borg, it was very much a case of "the older we get, the better we used to be".

Steve cursed a bit after committing the odd mistake, but stopped short of hurling his racket into space or decapitating any of the bunnies watching us from the nearby wood. I tried a few daring shots, yet somehow he managed to return nearly all of them. It was 1984 revisited as I blew a 5–2 lead in the first set to lose 7–6.

"You up for another one?"

Too bloody right I was. So off we went again and in no time I'd built up a 4–1 advantage. Two games away from making it one set all, then we'd be into a decider. Of course it didn't last. Steve began his traditional fight back and I lost the second as well, 6–4. I couldn't even blame defeat on the previous evening as my opponent had polished off just as much beer, if not more, than I had.

"You know that's exactly the way it always used to be," said Steve as we sat panting beside the court afterwards. "The longer the rally, the more frustrated you would get. I never had to hit winners against you. I just had to try and get the first few balls back, then wait for you to make a mistake."

"Hold on a minute. It wasn't *always* like that. I think I probably won more times against you than I lost."

"Maybe. But you didn't win today, did you? And you're only as good as your last match."

Thanks Steve.

I don't know when, or even if, we'll ever get round to doing it again. But it was fun. And, much to my relief, my crocked hand had stood up to a couple of hours of fairly competitive tennis. Which was just as well, considering what I'd let myself in for over the coming weeks.

I'd hoped Steve might be able to stick around after the match for a pint in one of Warnham's pubs. Sure, I wanted to catch up on things and talk about old times. But I was also desperate for somebody to, how can I put it, 'hold my hand' as I took my first look around the village since the days when I still had a full head of hair. However, he had other commitments (either that or I had been a complete wanker at school, and he couldn't bear to be around me anymore). So we took a few courtside snaps to mark the long-awaited reunion of two great Sussex sporting icons, and I drove him back to Horsham. We said our goodbyes, promising not to leave it so long next time.

Half an hour later I was back in Warnham, checking into my Bed & Breakfast in Church Street and trying to tell a confused Liz Cox about the background to my tennis trip.

"So you're swimming through England, right?" asked Liz.

"No, I'm playing tennis."

"But I thought you said something about swimming?"

"I did. A film called *The Swimmer* starring Burt Lancaster gave me the idea to do it."

"To swim?"

"No, to play tennis."

"Whatever. It must be wonderful to be back here after all this time. You'll be itching to get out and have a look around. I'll show you up to Sophie's room. Would you like a cooked breakfast in the morning?"

I said yes, though I hadn't a clue what I'd agreed to. My mind had gone completely blank after I'd heard the word *Sophie*. For some bizarre reason, I was getting seriously worked up about spending one night in a room once used by a girl I hadn't seen for more than 20 years, someone I never really knew that well anyway. I tried to convince myself that I'd merely checked into four walls surrounding some beautiful furnishings inside a to-die-for country cottage, which I had. But I couldn't, because there was Sophie's bed. There were her pictures on the wall, her books on the shelves, the mirror on the wardrobe door that she must have used to adjust her curly blonde hair a thousand times.

I took a shower in the bathroom that Sophie... well, you get the picture. Enough was enough – I had to get outside. I pulled on some clothes and walked into the late afternoon rain that had begun sweeping up from the English Channel. I passed the Vicarage and the new house beside it owned by Mr Lufthansa, the one built over the first tennis court I ever remember playing on. There was my old junior school, the village green and a balding Paul Tidy strolling along Freeman Road, looking just like his father did around 1980. Keen not to be recognised, I turned up my jacket collar and kept going.

Eventually, I came to what had once been our house, the white cottage shoehorned into the lowest point of the valley where Friday Street becomes Byfleets Lane. Through a window, I could see a man sitting at the table in the dining room, sipping what looked like a glass of red wine. He looked very at home. This was weird, how I imagine it would be to bump into your ex-wife – the love of your life who packed her bags after discovering your secret stash of Chris Evert photos – out on the town with her new man. I'd never realised people could get possessive about houses. Spouses and other halves, yes. Bricks and mortar, no.

I began drifting off into Hollywood mode (come on guys, we all do it) picturing myself as Robert de Niro, breaking down the back door, pulling a gun on wine-drinking man and in that unmistakably menacing Italian/New Jersey tone, booming, "How you doin'? You looking after her, eh? You looking after her? You fixed the roof, you painted the porch? You'd better or there'll be hell to pay. Do you hear me? Hell TO PAY!" And then calmly walking out again.

By now the rain was falling harder, running down my neck and soaking the newly-ironed shirt I'd put on barely an hour earlier. Yet even if it had been the balmiest Sussex-summer evening on record, I don't think I'd have wanted to stand there looking at the old place any longer.

That evening I went along to Evensong at the village church, not to pray for plenty of straight-sets wins on my journey, but to gawp at where I had once sung as a choirboy. Oh yeah, and to get me out of Sophie's room. I'd wanted to just sit at the back in the shadows, out of the way. Fat chance. Within seconds of finding a pew I'd been spotted by Vin Phillips, a reader at St Margaret's since the days of

Jonah and the whale. And as Vin would be leading us in tonight's service, he insisted I sat at the front as a special guest, where I was immediately recognised by a few others in the congregation. I don't know how. I had certainly never sported a leather jacket or an army haircut as a chorister.

After the service several people came over to say hi and find out what had brought me back to Warnham. Plenty of nods, smiles and "that's so interesting"s, but from the look on their faces the vast majority clearly thought I was depriving another village somewhere of an idiot. Vin said what a shock it had been to hear about my father, and as the subject of my mother came around again I opted once more for the tried-and-tested "she's very well, thanks," reply. Mrs Almond, once the toughest school dinner-lady in the south, told me her son was now in the Royal Air Force. This was incredible news. Ralph couldn't kick a football straight as an 11-year-old, so God only knows how he flies fighter planes.

And then everyone went their separate ways, them to their cosy homes and me to The Greets Inn for a quick pint. Once a favourite haunt of smugglers on their way to and from London and the south coast, The Greets was always the pub to be seen in down our end of the village. It was here, back in about 1984, that the actor Ronald Pickup – a *Jackanory* regular and brother of one of the locals – had bought me my first proper pint, little knowing I was still at secondary school. I remember the look on the landlord's face years later when, having established myself as a regular, I finally blew my cover on the night of my 18th birthday.

For someone wanting to keep a low profile, a trip to the pub probably wasn't the best of moves. But to me, going back to Warnham and avoiding The Greets would be like sightseeing in Moscow and missing out Red Square. By a stroke of luck, the place was empty except for three men, none of whom I recognised, standing together at the bar. I ordered a pint and found a perch in a dimly-lit corner to write up some notes covering Day One of the trip, then turned in.

Put it down to all the physical activity of the previous day, the nervous exhaustion of being back in Warnham or some kind of divine intervention after Evensong, but the ghost of Sophie Cox failed to stop me sleeping like a dead thing that night. It sounds corny, but in the morning I sat down for breakfast feeling like a man reborn, one finally at peace with his decision to write about, rather than become, Jimmy Connors. Those last-minute demons, the ones about revisiting a place full of happy memories synonymous with a time when my father was still alive, had been exorcised.

I'd just started on my eggs, bacon, beans and fried slice when an impossibly good-looking young couple entered the dining room and asked if they could join me. They were Germans, Franz and

29

Anna, over from Stuttgart to visit a pilot friend of theirs who lived locally. I wondered if they were here to see Mr Lufthansa, and whether I should take them to task for mixing with the man who helped destroy one of my childhood haunts. But in the interests of world peace and my new, soothed state of mind, I let it go.

Franz said they had been down to Warnham's other pub, The Sussex Oak, the night before and couldn't understand why the barman had rung a bell spot on 10.30, then asked them to drink up and leave. I told Franz this had been nothing personal, and was simply down to England's ridiculously out-of-touch licensing laws. And before I knew it, I was up to my neck in quick sand.

"I think it's got something to do with the First World War. The politicians didn't want people up all night drinking when there was a war on, so they made all the pubs shut by 11 o' clock, 10.30 on a Sunday. That way everyone was fit to fight the..."

Oh bollocks. There shouldn't have been any awkwardness. World War II was 60 years ago and bygones should be bygones. But there was. And then I made things worse by trying to crack a joke.

"So, in a funny way you did win the war, as back home you can stay out drinking much later, right?"

Complete silence. Grabbing a fork, I pushed an unwanted piece of fried tomato around my plate until it created a hole in the ground into which

I jumped. It seemed like the perfect time to pack my bags, say goodbye to Warnham and start my journey proper.

CHAPTER THREE

Leatherdead

**"The Martians could land in the car park and
no-one would care."**
Del Amitri, *Nothing Ever Happens*

So there I was, drifting through the country lanes
along the Sussex/Surrey border, just the Morris and
Kate Bush's piercing voice for company, eyes
scanning from left to right looking for courts and
unwitting victims to play.

Legend has it that Capel, the first village you
come to after leaving Sussex for Surrey on the A24,
was once the scene of a fierce battle between the
English and a mob of raping, pillaging Danes
(people, rather than the canine variety). Afterwards,
groups of local women, mad at the Danes for
choosing to pick on their men, are alleged to have
gone round and finished off every wounded
invader they could find with pitchforks. Then again

legend, in the words of comedian Billy Connolly, is nothing but rumour plus time, so I wouldn't believe everything you read on local tennis-club websites.

I parked the Morris outside Carter's General Store in the High Street and went inside to join the queue for some rather suspect-looking pasties in an oven beside the till.

"That'll be six pounds please," said the girl behind the counter in the style of a rapid-fire assault rifle.

"I beg your pardon?"

"Six pounds."

"What, for a pasty?"

"Oh, I thought you wanted to use the tennis courts, what with you dressed like that. You book them here. They're six pounds an hour. Pasties are 95p."

I handed over £6.95 in exchange for a pasty, a key attached to a piece of wood the size of a propeller on the Queen Mary, and directions to the courts. As I did so, a wave of guilt swept over me. I was already in danger of breaking one of the few, self-imposed rules that I'd set myself for the trip. It stated that *I could only stop and play on a court that I'd come across by chance, either from behind the wheel of the Morris or on foot.* In other words, driving around asking directions to the nearest one, then going to play on it, would be cheating. But I hadn't asked. Scary Shop Girl had done all the talking. So I reckoned I was marginally within the letter of the law. Anyway, sod it – I fancied a hit with someone.

"Will there be anybody down there to play against at this time of day?"

"This is a very expensive area. People don't have the time to play tennis."

I chewed Scary Shop Girl's reply over before attempting a response.

"So everyone works so hard to be able to afford to live here, that they're never actually around to enjoy the place, right?"

"Yeah, that's pretty much it. Everyone commutes to London or Dorking, then comes back in the evening by which time it's too late to go out and do anything."

I walked to the courts beside the village green trying to eat the pasty, balance my tennis bag and carry the propeller, all at the same time. Sure enough there wasn't a soul about, not even any potential tennis-playing dog walkers. I unlocked the gate, set my stopwatch to start counting down from 20 minutes, and began doing a few stretching exercises. Ten minutes passed and still there was no sign of Life on Capel. To kill time, I ambled over to the clubhouse beside the courts and peered through a window. I could see a large Roll of Honour covering the facing wall, containing the names of Capel Tennis Club champions dating back to the war. Someone called K. Mitchell appeared to have won the men's title the last six years running.

Perhaps that explained why I had nobody to play – he'd frightened all the other members off.

With my 20 minutes almost up, I took a ball and prepared to hit one serve before continuing north to wherever the next court might be. I'd fixed my sights on the opposite side of the net when something caught my eye. Eight figures had appeared in the distance across the green, coming towards me out of the faint heat haze, a bit like Omar Sharif's big entrance in *Lawrence of Arabia*, only without the camels, the desert and Peter O'Toole... all right, nothing like Omar Sharif's big entrance in *Lawrence of Arabia*.

As they came closer, I realised all were female (thankfully *sans* pitchforks) and dressed in tennis gear. One of them came straight over to me, presumably to find out why I was alone on a tennis court in Capel on a weekday afternoon, not slaving over an office desk in Whitehall like the rest of the village. I told her about my trek and she introduced herself as Mandy Tanswell, chairman of the tennis club. And yes, of course it was okay to have a hit with 'the girls'.

It emerged that I had gatecrashed their regular Monday afternoon tennis get-together, and upset the pre-arranged sides for two games of doubles in the process. But 'the girls' didn't seem to care. Quite the contrary if I was to take a blonde one called Carol at her word.

"I know – we'll all take it in turns with you. We

know how to tire a young man out. You'll be exhausted once we've all had our hands on you...!"

The other seven, up until then the epitome of home-counties afternoon-tea conservatism, suddenly began to "wey-hey" and "whoar" as though they had come face to face with Mr Universe, which my wife will assure you I am not. Having tried and failed to stop blushing, I replied that, as a married man with a little one on the way, the only thing I'd be unzipping that afternoon would be the cover on my tennis racket. This was greeted with jeers. Why the hell does stuff like that never happen to you when you're single?

I reckoned about an hour on the job with eight fit women was enough for any man, and in a major boost to my ego they declared themselves satisfied with my still somewhat-rusty performance. I said my farewells and Mandy suggested the name of a good tennis club I could look out for in nearby Dorking.

With not a baseline to be seen in the villages of Beare Green and Holmwood, Mandy's recommendation turned out to be my next port of call: nine beautifully-kept floodlit astroturf courts dotted around a posh clubhouse just to the south of Dorking town centre. But there was a catch. The people who lived here obviously had a touch of the Capel 'All Work No Play' Syndrome, as again there wasn't anyone about. This time no kinky groups of commuter-belt females turned up to save the day, so after 20 minutes I trudged over to Court Seven and struck, without doubt, the finest serve I'd hit in years – against the Invisible Man.

I'd imagined that Dorking, with its millionaire avenues and *Daily Telegraph* letter-writing types, would be loaded with tennis courts. I was wrong, but as the place seemed to be about as lively as Berlin on VE Day, I wasn't exactly gutted by their absence. I drove out of town towards Box Hill, Kate Bush having made way for Fleetwood Mac's *Rumours* on the car stereo and the first signs of sunburn staring back at me in the rear-view mirror.

Then it happened, amid the rolling North Downs countryside on the road to Leatherhead. I brought the Morris to a halt halfway across a pavement and jogged back a few yards to the gap in the fence through which I'd caught sight of it. And there it was – a tennis court in a back garden.

This was the moment I'd been dreading since setting out from Warnham. To play on a public court, you simply walk on and pay an attendant, should he or she start hassling you. To play at a private club, you just ask permission to join in. But a back garden is someone's very own private universe. They've worked hard to afford it. The court is there so they don't have to go to the local park and mix with the likes of you and me. Think about it. If you had one in your back yard, what would you do if a six-foot three skinhead knocked on your front door and asked to use it?

The court appeared to be inside the grounds of a three-storey Victorian mansion, which I realised on closer inspection had been divided into four separate houses. The only way to find out who owned it was to knock on each door. I parked the Morris and crunched my way up a long gravel driveway. The whole place stank of wealth. Tiptoeing around the Jaguars and BMWs scattered outside, I went up to the first front door. After about a minute, a well-presented woman in her mid-to-late forties answered, and I went into my well-rehearsed spiel – book, tennis, Sussex to Yorkshire, Burt Lancaster, this is not a robbery, would you like to have a rally with me on your court please?

"How absolutely fascinating, but it's not ours. It belongs to our neighbours next door and they're away. But I shouldn't think they'd mind."

Bingo – this was easier than I'd thought. I said thanks and followed her directions through a garden the size of Devon, only to find there were actually two courts – one in perfect condition surrounded by wire fencing, the other looking as though it hadn't been used since the days when Fred Perry last won Wimbledon. You can guess which one was padlocked to keep cretins like me out.

I tracked down Well-Presented Woman again and asked if she had a spare key for the good one. She didn't, which left me with no option but to play among the weeds and potholes of court number two. I took aim over where I thought the net had once stood and served, WPW having declined my offer of a quick rally. I couldn't say if the ball went in or not. The lines were barely visible, but it looked good. Mission accomplished, I walked back up the drive towards the Morris and continued north.

I'd already decided to spend that night in Leatherhead. Not because I'd heard it was some kind of Surrey tennis-court mecca but because I knew absolutely zip about the town. I arrived bang in the middle of rush-hour, so besides scouring the sides of each road for guest houses and tennis courts, I also had to deal with a thousand and one morons all playing 'Let's Cut The Morris Minor Up' in cars worth more than some entire Yorkshire streets.

It came as a massive relief when three courts came into view in the park outside the Leisure Centre, giving me an excuse to pull over and let the gel-haired, rubber-burning executive fuckwits find another make of car to pick on. I lay in wait for the first passer-by, a guy bearing a passing resemblance to Bob Hoskins. He was wearing odd shoes, one a black lace-up, the other a brown slip-on. As he drew level with the court I sprang and launched into my spiel. He listened to most of it, all the while eyeing the sports bag slung over my shoulder as though it contained rocket launchers rather than tennis rackets. I got as far as Burt Lancaster before he suddenly remembered the train he had to catch. Extreme fear in his eyes, I let him go.

I had better luck with Ben, walking home from his IT job, who willingly accepted my challenge. I handed him a racket and we hit for a few minutes, me in my tennis outfit, he in his suit and tie, much to the amusement of another player on an adjacent court, waiting for his opponent to turn up.

Ben retired, having been clocked and laughed at by a couple of work colleagues, after which I agreed to have a quick hit with the other guy who introduced himself as Colin.

"So what's Leatherhead famous for then, Colin?" I probed as we pinged a ball back and forth.

"Well, Anthony Trollope is meant to be buried close by, and I think Michael Caine lives locally. I've seen his wife down here."

"What, on these courts?"

"Ha ha! No, in town around the shops. Really, it's just the kind of place people pass through on their way to somewhere else, what with it being so close to the M25, and it's also a popular home for commuters working in London. But I'll be the first to admit that living here isn't exactly a thrill a minute."

Not the best public-relations pitch I've ever heard on behalf of one's home town, but nothing compared to the rant delivered by the landlady who welcomed me into The Swan Guest House about half an hour later.

"I call it Leatherdead. Nothing happens. Absolutely nothing. This building is due to be knocked down soon anyway, so I'm going to use that as my excuse to get out of here. Then there won't be any guesthouses around like this. Who can afford to live in a £300,000 house and get by charging people £30 a night to stay?"

But surely Leatherhead must have some good points?

"No, I can't say it has. But at least I get to meet some interesting people. Last night we had a man staying here who'd come all the way from Norway just to learn how to make truffles. Apparently there's some food research place round here that is going to teach him."

So there you have it. Leatherhead's offering to the world. Truffle-making.

That night I walked into the town centre to see if 'Leatherdead' really would live up to its name. I found an American-style diner, where the staff looked surprised rather than pleased to see me, and sat down at a table facing the window. And not one person walked past in the time it took for my food to arrive. I know because, being extremely sad, I kept an eye fixed on the pedestrianised precinct outside. Leatherdead made Dane-ravaged Capel look like Oxford Street on a Saturday in December.

As I went to pay for my chilli-burger and two beers, I asked one of the waitresses if the town was always this quiet during weekday evenings.

"Oh no. There's a big meeting going on at the theatre tonight. Something to do with the shops. I think everyone has gone there."

The Thorndike Theatre was only five doors away from the diner so, with bugger all else to do, I went see what all the fuss was about. A huge banner carrying the words 'Save Leatherhead' hung above the main entrance. It didn't say what from – boredom, loony tennis players, Mrs Caine's shopping sprees – but out of curiosity I went inside to the main auditorium where the local MP was busy addressing a standing-room-only crowd.

"What's going on?" I whispered to an official-looking woman at the back with a clipboard.

She placed a finger across her lips and led me by the arm through some double doors back out into the foyer. Then she began to talk. And talk. And talk.

"In the 20 years since this town was pedestrianised, almost 80 shops have been forced to shut resulting in more than 500 job cuts and a current unoccupancy rate of 20 per cent, which is 5 per cent above the national average, completely unacceptable for a town of almost 80,000 people and...", at which point my brain, bamboozled by statistics, began to fry.

Her gist appeared to be that pedestrianisation was an evil thing, right up there with Chile's civil-rights record, and traffic should be allowed back into the town to prevent it from dying. Oh,

43

and maybe I would consider making a small contribution of perhaps £10 to help fund the campaign? I stopped short of inviting her to rearrange the words 'must', 'be', 'joking' and 'you', and thanked her for the talk. Angry that I'd bothered to waste a night of my life in such a depressing place, I hurried back to my pokey little room at The Swan to salvage something from the evening – a couple of hours in front of the TV watching *Rocky III*.

Ah, the Rocky movies. Where would any of us be without them? To mortals like me, they save us when we're holed up in hotels in southern England waiting for the sun to come up. To Sylvester Stallone, they provided him with enough dough to afford divorces from women he met while, er, filming them. But to the American band Survivor – dodgy eighties haircuts and guitar riffs – Rocky meant their whole damned career. Remember *Eye Of the Tiger* and *Burning Heart*? Their only hits in Britain, both top five, both from Rocky films.

I'm almost ashamed to admit this but, as a kid, I had certain songs that I would use to fire me up while playing in tennis matches. And one of them was *Eye Of The Tiger*. These were records I knew off by heart that I'd store in my head, replaying them over and over again to spur me on, a bit like a mantra. Besides *Eye Of The Tiger* there was also Van Halen's *Jump*, *This Is Not A Love Song* by PIL, Killing Joke's *Love Like Blood* and, when I needed to relax and find my groove, *Time After Time* by Cyndi Lauper. They were the tracks that, when I became famous, the BBC would use to accompany footage of me conquering the world with a tennis racket.

For years afterwards I thought I'd been alone in doing this sort of thing until, during subsequent drunken conversations with other sports-minded friends, I realised nothing could have been further from the truth. Thousands of us really did spend hours in dreamland scoring the winner in a World Cup final to the strains of Elvis Costello's *Pump It Up*, or hitting the title-clinching forehand at Wimbledon to *Town Called Malice* by The Jam. And where exactly did it get us? The last time I looked through one of those All Time Top 100 British Sports Personalities lists I didn't see my name, or yours come to think of it.

A couple of weeks before setting out from Sussex, I'd confessed all this to Vince, an old school pal with a record collection of Fat Boy Slim proportions. Vince, bless his thinning locks, had gone away and put together a compilation tape called *Music To Smash Heads By* especially for my journey. Eleven songs designed to help me destroy whatever opposition dared get in my way. He'd even produced a tasteful cover for it, showing two gangsters in dark suits and shades trying to stave one another's heads in.

The morning after the Leatherdead experience, and desperate to get *Eye Of The Tiger* out of my head having stayed with *Rocky III* till the bitter end, I decided it was time to give Vince's tape its first airing. I found a deserted court tucked away beside quiet lane near Chessington, parked the Morris with its windows down, placed the cassette in the stereo and turned up the volume. For the next hour, I served alone in time to the kind of music that confused American teenagers play backwards, searching for the hidden message that says 'Jump in front of the 10.30 from Denver'. Songs that get about as close to most mainstream radio station play-lists as British women tennis-players come to Wimbledon finals.

Having listened to the whole tape, I selected two outstanding tracks as my own personal anthems for the trip – *Faster* by The Manic Street Preachers and Motorhead's old chestnut *Ace Of Spades*. Put a Donnay in his hands and the Pope would want to crack heads to these babies. Fired up, I drove north until I spotted a court at Chessington's King Edward Recreation Ground. And there I bumped into Ron, a 70-year-old asthmatic on his way to meet some friends at the Hook & Southborough Bowls Club. Poor old fella. With the combined power of The Manics, Motorhead and myself on the opposite side of the net, Ron didn't have a prayer in our best of five rallies match. I *murdered* him. But he didn't seem to take offence, and afterwards invited me to join him for a cup of tea at the bowls club next door.

"I suppose that's what tennis needs, someone like him," said Ron, pointing at the picture of David Beckham on the back page of the previous day's *Daily Mail*. "You've got Henman and that other fella, but that's about it, eh? And with all due respect to either of them, they don't exactly make you want to pick up a racket and play.

"It's the same with bowls. They've been trying to make it appeal to younger people for years. Imagine if Beckham gave up football tomorrow and took up bowls. Think about what that would do for our sport. Everyone would start playing it. All our prayers answered in the blink of an eye."

While Ron was giving me a guided tour of the clubhouse, complete with prehistoric gramophone and beaten up records by dead crooners, it began to rain outside. Proper hard rain, the type that always jumps out at you from behind a tree when you're halfway between your house and the shops without an umbrella. The sky grew steadily darker. It was only mid-afternoon, yet outside cars were driving on full headlights.

We'd just arrived at the trophy cabinet when the door flew open to reveal a soggy-looking man, who Ron introduced as Fred. Fred had spent all morning mowing the greens, and was now looking forward to a packed lunch washed down with some music.

"Harry Secombe anyone?"

And before I could spit out the words "Depends if you want to find yourself six feet under in the

near future," Fred had *This Is My Song* spinning on
the turntable, a tune with a built-in gismo designed
to make you puke after 0.53 seconds. I thanked
Ron for his hospitality and hurried back to the
Morris, getting drenched in the process.

After an hour reading a copy of *The Surrey
Advertiser* in the car, heater on full-blast in a vain
attempt to dry out, I decided to call Steve Appleton
– tennis player, all-round nice bloke and my uncle.
We'd made tentative plans to meet that evening for
a game at his local club in Surbiton, which just
happened to be in the direction I was heading. But
with the football pitch in front of me fast turning
into a lagoon, that wasn't going to happen unless
we could find a leisure centre willing to lend us
some armbands.

We agreed to do the only sensible thing –
postpone the tennis until the following morning
and go to the pub instead. I dropped the Morris off
at his house and after a bite to eat courtesy of my
Aunt Jill, we walked to The North Star on Hook
Road to take part in the Tuesday night pub quiz.
I might not have a clue what year Thomas Becket
was murdered, or who John the Baptist's mother
was, but I know which sport Todd Woodbridge
plays, so I was made to feel welcome by the other
members of 'The Judean People's Front.' We came
a close second to 'Wenger's Barmy Army' and split
our £10 runners-up prize four ways. Better than a
smack in the mouth with a wet fish I suppose, even

if £2.50 wasn't even enough to cover the cost of one pint of lager.

So the rain-enforced break in play worked out pretty well after all. I got to enjoy some home cooking, down a few drinks in the company of a familiar face and spend the night at my aunt and uncle's cosy semi-detached. Beats burger and chips, a pint on your own, then back to a damp-smelling guesthouse anytime.

Steve and I played our match the following morning at the Surbiton Hill Methodist Tennis Club, popular in these parts for its cheap membership rates rather than any kind of hotline to the Big Man upstairs. And I won. No mean feat, as although Steve may be the wrong side of 60, he still plays two or three times each week. Which is two or three times more than I played in the five years leading up to April 2002.

The rain clouds of the previous day had vanished and I was on a winning streak of two matches, *Ace of Spades* blasting from the car stereo as I edged my way through suburbia towards the spiritual home of lawn tennis – Wimbledon.

CHAPTER FOUR

The Wild Card

"I don't think I really came to appreciate what royalty meant to you Brits until I came to Wimbledon, with all its pomp and circumstance."
John McEnroe

Right then, it's confession time. Cast your mind back to the very beginning and my night out in Horsham with the Grade Twos. Remember how I told them I hadn't planned a route for my trip, that I just wanted to go where the wind and the Morris took me?

Well I'm afraid that was only 99 per cent true. The remaining one per cent had the name of one town written all over it, somewhere I always intended to visit. I ask you. How can you go on a tennis-inspired journey from southern to northern England and not pass through Wimbledon?

Wimbledon. Probably the most famous tennis tournament in the world, and still the one the majority of professional players want to win above all others. Home to strawberries, cream, a permanent low-pressure weather system and 18 of the finest grass courts in the world including the mother of them all, the Centre Court. What was the likelihood of The All England Lawn Tennis & Croquet Club, to give the place its full title, letting me hit a ball or two on one of them?

A sixth sense told me that if I just appeared from out of the blue and tried to play, then the powers that be would have me in Wimbledon Nick faster than it takes to say "The ball was good, Mr McEnroe." So four months before I planned to set off from Sussex, I wrote a polite letter to the Chief Executive, Christopher Gorringe, explaining all about my trip and asking if he'd be so good as to let me serve one ball on the Centre Court. Just one, measly little serve. A couple of weeks later, to my surprise, I got a reply. And this is what it said.

> *Dear Mr Vignes*
>
> *Certainly your project is an interesting and novel one. Whilst the All England Club might be able to help you it will, however, be dependent upon timing in view of the preparations for the Championships. Even if we were to help, I am afraid the Centre Court or any of the other main show courts would have to be ruled out.*

In the meantime, I would be grateful if you could let me know which other major clubs in the country have given their written agreement to your playing on any of their courts.

Yours sincerely

Christopher Gorringe

Chief Executive

I don't know about you, but at first glance that seems quite encouraging. Now read it through again, paying extra attention to the bits that follow the word 'even'. Not quite so promising, eh? No Centre Court or 'other main show courts' and a vague attempt to keep up with the Joneses at the end. One friend I showed the letter to for a second opinion said Mr Gorringe may as well have written

Dear Mr Vignes

You've got to be joking.

Yours sincerely

and left it at that.

Unperturbed, I wrote back giving details of when I thought I'd be in the Wimbledon area, which was well in advance of the traditional Championship fortnight that spans the final week in June and the first in July. I tried a bit of flattery, saying that because of the spontaneous 'turn-up-and-play' theme to my trip, the All England was in the unique position of being the only club I would be contacting in advance for permission. Finally, I pointed out that in 1877 the first man ever to win a Wimbledon Championship had been a chap called Spencer Gore, so it might be nice to let his namesake realise a lifelong dream of hitting a ball on one of the courts.

Then I waited. No response. Two weeks before I left Yorkshire for Sussex I wrote for a third and final time. Still nothing. And that was that. Perhaps they just hoped I'd eventually give up trying and go away. Well, I'm sorry, Mr Gorringe, but that was never going to happen. Come the time, I would have to resort to guerrilla tactics to get my way.

The drive from Surbiton to Wimbledon proved to be pretty uneventful, just a couple of public courts in New Malden and Raynes Park where I rallied with Lorna, out walking with her four-year-old son Liam, and a schoolboy called Nathan who tried to pocket two balls without me noticing. Stupid child. If he'd asked, I would have given them to him. But he didn't, so I went for maximum embarrassment potential by asking him to turn his pockets out. Which, I've got to admit, the school-master in me really enjoyed.

I arrived outside the All England Club a little after 3pm, three hours before I'd arranged to meet up with Rab, an old friend with a wicked sense of humour who had agreed to help me wreak my revenge on the suits of SW19. To pass the time

I took a walk around the Wimbledon Museum, which proved to be £5.50 extremely well spent. McEnroe's shoes from 1985, Borg's racket from 1981, Pat Cash's headband from 1987 and a lovely picture of Anna Kournikova unfastening her bra on Court One in 2000. Sorry, wishful thinking that last one (note to museum organisers – might be worth getting hold of anyway in case you ever need to bump those visitor numbers up).

Worth the entrance fee alone was some fantastic grainy film from around the turn of the century of people playing 'stationary' tennis. I use the word 'stationary' as nobody ever seemed to move. They just stood there rooted to the spot, hitting the ball backwards and forwards, breaking sweat only when absolutely necessary. Like the time someone resembling David Niven shouted "Pimms up, Ginny" from the sidelines.

Afterwards, I drove back into Wimbledon town centre to meet Rab outside the railway station. We went to a pub on the Common (of Wombles' fame) called The Hand In Hand, and I took him through my plan to get one over on the All England Club and hit a ball on one of their courts after all.

"I've looked at the maps, and the closest court to a road is Court Two," I explained, for no apparent reason adopting the clipped wartime tones of Richard Attenborough in *The Great Escape*. "From Somerset Road I reckon it is just about possible to hit a ball over the stand directly onto the court. That way I can say that I've hit a ball on the grass at Wimbledon. But there are two potential problems."

"Go on."

"First, it's right by a security gate. Second, because of that the shot has to be a good one. I'll probably get two goes, no more, before security realise what's going on and try to stop me."

"Right. So where do I come in?"

"Rab, I want you to be the getaway driver. I want the car to be right there, engine running so I just have to hit the shot, jump in and get the hell out of there."

By now Rab was virtually crying with laughter. Not at my Richard Attenborough impersonation, but at the thought of being a getaway driver in a Morris Minor.

"Okay, you've got yourself a getaway driver, but I'm gonna need to have a quick test drive to work out how that bloody thing works, all right?"

From my bag I took the thick black marker pen bought specially for the occasion and began scribbling a message to Chris Gorringe on a tennis ball. I wrote 'Spence's Wild Card – 1/5/02' before adding a churlish, but I felt appropriate, 'Thanks For Nothing'.

As dusk fell, Rab test-drove the Morris back to the All England Club. We pulled up in Somerset Road in the shadow of Court Two, close to Wimbledon's Gate 13. With Fat Boy Slim's remix of The Rolling Stones' *Satisfaction* playing on the car stereo I got out, walked to the middle of the road, bounced the ball once on the tarmac and clobbered it high into the evening sky. It cleared the spectator stand with something to spare and fell into the space occupied by the grass. A direct hit. I jumped into the car and we sped away, nought to 40 miles an hour in two minutes over three sets of speed bumps.

"Very smooth," said Rab.

With a bit of help from a friend, I'd managed in a roundabout way to hit a ball on Court Two at Wimbledon. But over the coming days I developed something of a brooding resentment at the All England Club over what had happened. Of course they'd had more important things to worry about, like organising one of the biggest tennis tournaments in the world for starters. But had one serve really been too much to ask for, even on one of the less fashionable outside courts? In my darker moments I couldn't help wondering if someone somewhere had noticed I didn't wear the right school tie, spoke with a slight accent, or simply wrote for *The Guardian* rather than *The Times*. Had I been a victim of the old adage that it's not who you are, but who you know, which still applies as much today in many British sporting circles as it did a century ago? Paranoia perhaps, but after five pints of strong bitter the mind runs ragged.

I spent that night on the couch at the getaway driver's flat in south-west London, sparing me the problem of finding a Bed & Breakfast in the Wimbledon area costing less than a Premier League footballer's weekly wage for a one-night stay. Rab woke me, as requested, as he left for work around 7.30am.

"Checked Teletext to see if anyone was killed by a flying tennis ball in Wimbledon last night?"

I laughed, told him where to go, waited for the sound of the front door opening and shutting, then made a lunge for the TV remote control. The morning headlines contained no mention of any elderly All England Club members being hit on the head with fatal consequences while out for an evening stroll around Court Two. Funny how fast you can wake up when you've got a guilty conscience.

After careful thought, I decided to break with tradition for the next leg of my trip by ditching the Morris and taking to my feet. The lethal combination of trying to negotiate London's busy streets while searching for tennis courts made me realise that sooner or later I was bound to:

a) run someone over

b) smash the Morris up

c) spot a court, but waste at least a day searching for a parking place

d) all of the above.

As a great believer in people, a no-claims bonus stretching back to 1986 and the value of time, walking seemed a better option.

I left the Morris at the getaway driver's and caught the tube out to Wimbledon Park, the nearest stop to the All England Club, to pick up from where I'd left off the previous night. To avoid returning to the scene of the crime, I took a slight detour across a golf course in the direction of Southfields, stopping briefly to have a quick knock with Dan and John, two Canadian lads playing on a public court. After a couple of rallies I left them to it, aware of the strong vibes coming my way which seemed to say "Can't you see we're in the middle of a match here – piss off!"

By lunchtime I'd found an internet café in Putney and decided to put my feet up for an hour or so, down a couple of nice but harshly priced whipped-cream mocha-type things and check my emails. Bit of a mixed bag – one from a Grade Two asking if I was still alive, another from a friend slumming it in Australia, a couple of work commissions that would have to wait and a simple 'Hiya' from 'Alex & Bump', which caused me to well up. Not the done thing when you're prowling the streets of London doing your best impression of a serious athlete.

Composure regained, I logged on to the website of the Lawn Tennis Association, the sport's governing body in Great Britain, to do a bit of research. Lots of words like 'development', 'commitment', 'sponsorship' and 'youth' together with a 'Frequently Asked Questions' section.

I looked for the one that said '*What am I doing reading this when my destiny was to conquer the tennis world, become a rich bastard and share a bed every night with Cindy Crawford and Sheryl Crow*', but couldn't find it anywhere.

Then it suddenly dawned on me – the LTA's headquarters were at Queen's Club, home of the pre-Wimbledon Stella Artois Championships and only about two miles away from where I was sitting sipping coffee. Sorry, 'whipped-cream mocha'. Following the farce that had been my 'visit' to the All England Club, I knew I had to go. My only dilemma was whether I should call ahead and ask if they'd let me play, or just beg when I got there?

I took out a coin, chose heads for the turn-up-and-hope option, and flipped it onto the table beside my internet terminal. It landed tails. I took out my mobile phone, called the LTA number listed on the website and asked to be put through to the press office. Within five minutes I'd been given the okay to hit at Queens the following day. Not only that, but a press officer had also been assigned to find me somebody to play. After my string of futile letters to the All England Club earlier in the year, I didn't know whether to laugh or cry.

No change from a tenner for 45 minutes on the internet and two hot drinks is exactly the kind of reason why my wife and I left London for Yorkshire in 1999, but I'll come back to that little moan later. Poorer but distinctly more upbeat, I crossed the

River Thames at Putney Bridge and walked in the direction of Craven Cottage, home of Fulham Football Club, through Bishop's Park. My A to Z map of London said I'd find public tennis courts here. I expected three, maybe four but certainly not 15. And they all seemed to be in use.

I stood at the entrance of some rickety changing rooms, sizing up who I should go and challenge. Slowly my eyes wandered to the notice board on the wall beside me, covered from top to bottom in messages from lonely tennis players with names like Albertine, Orvil, Dolores and Vipin, all desperately seeking other tennis players. I suppose they all wanted to meet up to play tennis, but from some it was hard to tell. Try this one...

'South African man, mid-20s, looking for regular weekend partners, either sex – any standard welcome.'

And if you think I'm making this up, go to Bishop's Park and see for yourself.

Taking care to avoid any male looking remotely South African, I ambled round to court nine where Sarah, a '*keen but lousy*' tennis player (her words, not mine), was being coached by a guy called Chris. I watched the two of them going through their practice drills for a few minutes before interrupting, doing my spiel and asking Chris for permission to have a quick hit with his pupil.

The two of us rallied for a while with me standing at the net hitting balls to Sarah's forehand, allegedly one of her weaker shots. It soon became apparent that Sarah wasn't half as lousy as she'd said she was, and with the afternoon sun beating down beads of sweat began to trickle down my forehead into my eyes, stinging my contact lenses.

"You've played quite a bit before, haven't you?" said Chris as he watched us from the tramlines. Unsure at first whether he was actually talking to me, I nodded in return. I mean, who am I to argue with a qualified coach?

Keen to plough on towards Hammersmith, I left Bishop's Park and began walking up Fulham Palace Road, a grin the size of the Thames barrier on my face thanks to Chris's backhanded compliment. At the end of my first week on the road I certainly felt fitter, and after years in tennis 'retirement' it was good to know that someone else thought I looked the part. My only regret so far was that – the two Steves apart – I wasn't getting any competitive matches, just a series of knock-ups against people convinced they were being conned into appearing on some kind of candid camera TV show.

That all changed the next day when, as arranged, I reported for duty at Queen's Club following a second night on the getaway driver's couch.

Queen's is the strangest of places, a block of land at the end of a narrow terraced street in one of the most expensive areas to live in Britain, if not the world. Imagine Berkshire's poshest country club being sucked up by a tornado and dumped 40 miles away in the big smoke near the Hammersmith Flyover. It looks that out of place.

The wonderfully-named Amber Hinde at the LTA press office had asked me to be at the main reception around 1pm to meet Matt Sprake, the opponent she had found for me. I arrived early and decided to kill 15 minutes having a snoop around. Peering over a wall in the car park, I came face to face with a couple having stand-up sex against a tombstone in the adjoining Hammersmith Cemetery. Temporarily bamboozled, I acknowledged them with a cheery "All right?". Stupid question really, given the circumstances, but what else was I going to say – "Anyone for tennis?"?

Praying that I hadn't just caught Matt Sprake with his trousers down, I walked briskly away and sat down on the veranda outside the main clubhouse to read a newspaper. A few feet away a man in a tracksuit stood talking on a mobile phone. As he turned to face me I realised it was Roger Taylor, a Wimbledon semi-finalist in 1970 and now captain of the Great Britain Davis Cup team, the tennis equivalent to manager of a national football team. I waited for him to finish his call, then said hello.

"Are you planning on going through Sheffield?" he asked after I'd told him why I was visiting Queen's. "If you do, go to Weston Park. That's where I started playing as a kid, on the public courts near the university. Do me a favour. If they're still there, will you let me know?"

I said I would, providing I made it to Sheffield, and we shook hands.

"Are you Spencer?" said a voice behind me as I made a note of Roger's request in my notebook. It was Matt Sprake, and thankfully he wasn't the bonking man.

"I've booked one of the practice courts for our match. We've only got around an hour and a half, so we'd better get started."

The bad news was the practice court had a hard surface, not grass. I'd been looking forward to playing on the green stuff that Queens – like Wimbledon – is famous for. But with the Stella Artois Championships only a month away, they were being tended for the likes of Hewitt and Henman rather than Morris Minor-driving drifters.

Matt was working on a temporary contract in the LTA's membership department, and had spent most of the previous month playing God over which members should get Wimbledon tickets for the 2002 tournament. In his mid-twenties and, like me, something of a lapsed player, he was also making the most of his time at Queen's by playing at lunchtimes and after work, trying to get his game back up to scratch.

We found our court and began warming up. The bounce of the ball seemed extremely high, probably because this was a decent court unlike the public park wrecks I'd spent most of my time playing on so far. Matt won the toss, elected to serve and we began, me eager to make a good impression during my first and probably last appearance at Queen's. On my toes, eye on the ball, bandana wrapped around my forehead to keep the sweat from my eyes, Manic Street Preachers flooding through my veins.

At 0–3 down in the first set I couldn't see a way back. Matt was on form and despite playing some good shots, I hadn't come close to winning a game. At the change of ends we took a quick break, during which Matt leaned in to whisper something to me.

"Have you seen who's playing beside us?"

I hadn't. I glanced over at the two players who had just started knocking up on the court adjacent to ours. It was Martin Lee and Jamie Delgado, the British numbers three and four of the moment. Their world rankings may have been 95 and 156, but up close they looked awesome.

Neither Matt or I said anything but from the first serve of the next game we both started playing out of our skins, desperate not to be shown up by the professionals next door making the whole thing look so effortless. Our next six games took almost an hour to complete with plenty of rallies, deuces, advantage points and blown advantage points. Roger Taylor arrived to cast an eye over Martin and Jamie and, if I'm not mistaken, definitely looked in our direction on a few occasions. It was exhausting yet exhilarating stuff. At 33, a veteran's age in today's tennis world, I was finally getting the opportunity to show British tennis what it had been missing. Tim who? It felt like my 15 minutes had arrived.

I eventually lost the first set 3–6, at which point Matt announced that he had to go back to work. I was gutted. I felt like I could carry on all afternoon, but with nobody around to play I was forced to call it a day. I thanked him for his time, and he went back to deciding which LTA members would be tucking into strawberries and cream at Wimbledon.

I suppose I could have challenged Martin or Jamie to a quick set, but with qualification for the French Open at Roland Garros just days away, I don't suppose either would have wanted to be shown up by my rapidly improving game.

My Queen's adventure over by mid-afternoon, I found myself at a bit of a crossroads. Should I give my right elbow and shoulder a well-earned break after seven days of straight tennis, or carry on walking through West London looking for courts? With my heart still pumping from the set against Matt, I plumped for the latter. I'd also left my change of clothes back at the getaway driver's, and didn't fancy traipsing round the Tate Gallery in sweat-drenched tennis gear.

I crossed the A4 dual carriageway, skirted round the outside of Hammersmith Broadway and found four courts in a trendy-looking London backwater called Brook Green, all tree-lined terraced avenues and the like. Spiel at the ready, I approached a guy with a ponytail practising serving on his own. His name was Johan, and his opponent had stood him up at short notice. He accepted my challenge and we went into a best-of-three-sets match, which I won 2–1. Sitting on a park bench afterwards sharing a bottle of water, I admitted that had probably been my best performance in years. My serve, forehand, volleying, even the unreliable backhand had all come together, *Ace of Spades* and *Faster* on a continual loop in my head. What's more, I hadn't panicked when Johan fought back from 4–1 down to 4–4 in the final set.

Little did I know, but I would come to regret my decision to carry on playing that day. And there would be nothing Motorhead or The Manics could do to help me.

CHAPTER FIVE

Ice Buckets & Elbows

"I was the most miserable I ever was in my five years there."
Ian Dury on his school days in High Wycombe

Mid-morning, Shepherd's Bush Common, on court with three South Korean students and their brand new, shiny rackets. The standard of play is poor and the language barrier colossal, but we're having a laugh. Lord knows what they make of me. They don't seem to have heard of Pete Sampras, let alone Burt Lancaster.

On the court beside us, three men and a woman are doing their best to have a serious doubles match, nigh on impossible when balls from our amateurish knock-up keep rolling under their feet. A mother arrives with four children and hands them plastic rackets. They start to play in the junction where the two nets meet. Twelve people, all of varying age and ability, attempting to play tennis on two courts. Completely ludicrous, yet nobody complains. Very British.

"This spor' velly good," says one of the Koreans, a girl called Jeong-Hee Yun. "Football and baseball only in South Korea. This much better. More fun, more fun."

I nod in agreement and shape up to take a serve. In the split second when the ball is in the air and my eyes are off the court, one of the children runs across the area I'm aiming for. The serve comes tearing down at around 70 miles per hour and clips the boy's trailing leg. Both mother and child are completely oblivious to what has nearly happened, but my heart is pounding. It's time to get back to the Morris before somebody here loses an eye.

I've got this cock-eyed theory that might just explain why the British are, with one or two glorious exceptions, crap at tennis. It's nothing to do with social class, under-investment or the weather. It's all about serving. And it goes something like this. Imagine you are a kid. You're given your first tennis racket and find a few friends to play against. You go to a court and begin knocking up. It's enjoyable. After a while you decide to play a match, which means someone has to serve. You have a go. It always looks easy on TV when the stars do it. But you soon discover it isn't. On the few occasions your racket does connect with the ball, it ends up flying in completely the wrong direction. You look like a prat. Rowing an aircraft carrier across the Pacific Ocean with a matchstick for a paddle would be easier. One by one your friends also discover that it's not as easy as Lleyton Hewitt makes it seem. You all lose interest and bugger off to do something else.

Serving is arguably the hardest opening move there is to any kind of sport. To start a football match, one player kicks a ball a few inches forward to another. Simple as that. In track events, the athlete waits for the word "Go" or the sound of a gun, then runs or walks off. But tennis is different. Each point begins with the server attempting to hit a ball over a net into a square the size of a postage stamp (at least that's what it looks like from the back of a court), keeping their feet behind a line as they do so. You're given two opportunities to get it right, it's that bloody difficult. It takes a lot of hard work and patience to perfect, something many kids in today's spoiled-for-choice consumer Britain don't have. Why bother standing in the rain learning how to serve when you can do it in the comfort of your own home on a computer game?

Little Ben, out walking with his mother across Latymer Upper School Playing Fields near Wormwood Scrubs, did his best to prove my theory correct. I handed him a racket and, for what seemed like an eternity, he tried to serve a ball. It was painful to watch, not just for me but also his mum, desperate to get to the shops before she died of starvation. Throwing the ball into the air above his head was easy. But raising the racket in time to hit it was something else altogether. In the end it all got too much and he burst into tears. I felt terrible. In the space of one hour I'd gone from almost decapitating one child with a serve to showing another exactly why he would never win Wimbledon.

The north-west suburbs of London proved to be a dead loss for tennis courts. Places like Willesden and Harlesden, full of railway yards and industrial estates called things like 'The Concord Zone'. Hassled by large trucks bearing the names of Polish fridge manufacturers, I could tell the Morris was just itching to leave the city behind and see some greenery. Together we moseyed from street to street heading west, eventually discovering one battered court, bereft of net, not far from the Hoover factory in Perivale. After a 15-minute wait, an attention-seeking tabby cat showed up. With no humans anywhere in sight, I challenged it to a game. It accepted, and I gently hit a ball underarm across the broken tarmac. Tabby scuttled away, brought it to a halt with a pounce, rolled around a bit in the dirt, got bored and walked off. Don't get me wrong – I love cats. But after the high of Queen's Club, this was back down to earth with a vengeance.

And then the previous evening's three-setter against Johan, together with the combined effect of eight days wear and tear on my right arm, caught up with me. Tennis Elbow affects thousands of people in

Britain every year, many of whom have never picked up a tennis racket in their lives. Bricklayers' Elbow would probably be more accurate. The physiotherapist who helped me recover from my football injury calls it *"the inflammation of the common extensor tendons in the elbow caused by repeated minor trauma, particularly through gripping"*. My definition when it first reared its ugly head in Ruislip was a touch more colourful than that.

I'd discovered a couple of courts on land leased by the Ministry of Defence to the American Air Force. The place was incredible, a mini US village deep in the heart of Middlesex with houses, a school, social club and sports facilities including a full-size baseball pitch, all used by forces staff and their families now based in the London area. Having been given 'clearance' to be on site by the brick outhouse-sized soldier on duty at the gym, I'd started rallying with a local policeman-come-part-time tennis coach by the name of Jim Taylor. After only a couple of minutes it became obvious something was wrong. I simply couldn't hit a ball straight to save my life. They were going everywhere, including high over the fence surrounding the courts. My right arm felt as though it had been yanked off, stripped of all tissue and bone, filled with jelly and stitched back on again.

I knew instantly what it was. I'd suffered briefly from tennis elbow around the age of 20, and remembered the jelly sensation that first signalled its arrival all too well. I made my excuses to Jim and, in a mild state of panic, went and sat in the Morris. What did this mean? Had I reached the end of the road already, barely a quarter of the way from Warnham to Normanton? Should I rest for a couple of days and see what happened, or give up and go straight home? Part of me was angry with myself for overdoing it and not taking more rest breaks. Playing tennis for long periods each day after so long away from the sport had been a recipe for disaster.

In an attempt to salvage the whole trip, I came up with a short-term plan – go to the nearest supermarket, buy some ice, pack it around my elbow, find somewhere decent to stay, feet up for a couple of days. No worries tracking down a supermarket and some ice, but I ended up driving another 10 miles into Buckinghamshire before discovering a Bed & Breakfast with a spare room. And along the way I passed two more tennis courts. Thankfully both were in the middle of nowhere, and I was left in peace for 20 minutes before hitting my one serve. Both weak, underarm efforts that barely cleared the net.

By the time I checked into the Mill View Guest House in High Wycombe it was already early evening. Morale low, I swapped my tennis garb for jeans and a t-shirt and went straight round to The Disraeli, a local pub I'd been told did good food. Finding a perch at the bar, I ordered chilli con carne and a pint. Without thinking, I leant forward on my elbows and a bolt of pain shot up my right arm causing me to wince. One of the barmaids, spotting my discomfort, asked what was wrong.

I gave her an abbreviated version of the whole sorry story.

"Not to worry love. We might have just what the doctor ordered. You stay there and I'll be back in a minute."

I started sipping my pint, expecting her to return with some kind of exotic pain antidote better known in the Greek islands as 'One Hundred Per Cent Flame Thrower'. So you can imagine my surprise and delight when she returned with an ice bucket loaded, funnily enough, with ice.

"Plonk your arm in that."

I switched the John Smiths to my left-hand side and did as I was told. Intrigued by the barmaid's alternative first-aid skills, a couple of middle-aged drinkers by the name of Sid and Chris came over to chat. Having decided to spend the following day away from tennis courts, I asked them what they would do given 24 hours to kill in High Wycombe.

"Go to the station and take the train to London," said Sid.

"I wouldn't go that far," said Chris, "but there's nothing really round here. I'd probably go out to West Wycombe. Nice place, good pubs. You could go and see where that mad bloke shagged all those women."

A baffling, yet inspired answer.

Seriously in the dumps and by now considering pulling the plug on the whole journey, I walked back to my room, chilli stains down my jeans where I'd tried and failed to eat left-handed. On TV, a shadowy figure was trying hard to bump off Whitney 'Why Stick To One Note When You Can Hit 17' Houston. Kevin Costner, stupid man, was attempting to stop him. I popped one of the painkillers bought earlier in the day from the supermarket in Ruislip. Tennis elbow or no tennis elbow, extreme measures are needed when the only channel in your room with decent reception is showing *The Bodyguard*.

I awoke the following morning to the sound of rain beating against my window. A quick peek outside revealed puddles everywhere and patches of mist covering the nearby hills. Even if my elbow had been 100 per cent, it would still have been too wet to play tennis.

Over breakfast I chose to follow Chris's advice and spend the day on the trail of this mad shagging bloke. Back in the 1750s, Sir Francis Dashwood returned from his Grand Tour of Europe and the Ottoman Empire and decided to recreate elements of what he'd seen abroad in his native West Wycombe. Eager for somewhere discreet to meet with his high-society mates, he employed local farm workers to build a series of caves in the chalk hill to the north of the town. On completion, Dashwood gave his gentleman's group a name – The Hellfire Club.

The club met regularly to play cards, drink, entertain a constant stream of women and, so the story goes, carry out the odd satanic ritual. Once the novelty of caves wore off, Dashwood had a large, hollow, golden ball constructed and fitted it to the top of St Lawrence Church overlooking West Wycombe. Big enough to fit six people, the ball provided him and his chums with splendid views of the surrounding landscape during their orgies. As though a man needs any distractions while attempting to satisfy three women at the same time.

"We get all sorts visiting here, from pop bands playing small shows to people who say they belong to other Hellfire Clubs around the world," said the woman selling refreshments and admission tickets at the entrance to the caves. "Unfortunately, there's no real proof of what the original Hellfire Club got up to. All the records were destroyed during the Victorian era. But there are all sorts of tales that seem to have been passed on by word of mouth."

"About group sex in the golden ball and the devil-worshipping stuff?"

"Um, that sort of thing, yes. Horrible weather for May, isn't it?"

I paid my £3.75 and went in. After spending the best part of ten days in the great outdoors, it felt strange being underground accompanied by a piped commentary (featuring the entire contents of the

BBC sound-effects department) and life-size model figures that all seemed to resemble Spike Milligan. Standing alone in what Dashwood had referred to as 'the Banqueting Hall', my mind began to return to the elbow problem. It felt okay now, but what would happen tomorrow when it came to picking up a racket again? If I continued like this, spending one day on the court and the next off, I wouldn't get home for months. And with Alex reaching the halfway mark in her pregnancy, that wasn't an option.

A phone call to my physio in Yorkshire that morning had confirmed my worst fears – that if I carried on playing, I could permanently damage the elbow. Some kind of protective strapping also seemed out of the question, because I'd still be bending my arm and aggravating any injury. Deep beneath the Buckinghamshire countryside, I made a pact with myself. If it still felt awkward the next time I hit a ball, the journey would be over. Having spent months worrying about whether the elderly Morris would make it, I was now the one in danger of throwing a spanner in the works.

More painkillers, an afternoon watching Humphrey Bogart in *High Sierra*, then a couple of hours writing notes covering Days Nine and Ten of what seemed on the verge of becoming a broken dream. Called Alex and told her what I planned to do. Apparently, I'll need my elbows to do some lifting towards the end of the year, so I ought to look after them. Packed a towel with ice, wrapped it around the affected area, settled down to watch Rocky IV. Fell asleep fully clothed and woke up hours later, water everywhere, thinking I'd wet myself. Towelled down and moved to the dry side of the double bed. Couldn't get back to sleep. Lay there in the dark, brain in knots, a John McEnroe circa 1981 voice chipping away in my head.

"*What are you doing here? Go home to your wife. Stop whining about your elbow and start acting like a normal person, you jerk.*"

– "I know, I know, but I've waited so long to do this and I've come this far. One more day John, that's all, just to see how it feels."

"*What difference is one more lousy day going to make? So your elbow feels all right in the morning. What's to stop it flaring up again in the afternoon? And don't call me John. It's Mr McEnroe to you.*"

– "Sorry. I suppose you're right."

"*You bet I'm right! Look, you're not exactly Burt Lancaster, Bill Bryson or even me for that matter. This idea of yours sucks. You're the pits, man. Go back to Yorkshire and leave this game to the big boys.*"

– "Get lost McEnroe."

"*WHAT?*"

– "You heard. Anyway, I was talking to myself!"

I didn't have far to go to discover whether the small glacier I'd worked through over the previous 36 hours had done the trick. High Wycombe Lawn Tennis Club was visible from the upstairs rear windows at the Mill View Guest House. I'd spotted it within minutes of arriving, but decided against making a visit until I'd given the elbow a chance to sort itself out.

Breakfast over, I climbed back into my tennis gear and went off in search of someone to hit with. Being a bank holiday there were kids everywhere, being supervised by half-a-dozen adults. I approached one, did the spiel, and was in turn introduced to a man in his twenties standing outside the clubhouse. His name was Paul Delgado, brother of Jamie Delgado, the guy I'd been playing next to at Queen's Club. Small world or what?

Paul had been hired by the club a couple of months earlier to do some coaching with the junior and adult members. Despite having another tennis appointment in Maidenhead later that morning, he agreed to rally with me for a few minutes before he had to leave. I explained about my elbow, and asked him to go easy while I established whether I'd be fit enough to play.

Heart in mouth, I bounced a ball and half-volleyed it down the court towards Paul. Back it came to my forehand. Here was the moment of truth. My racket connected. No pain, no twinge, no jelly elbow. I hit a second shot, then a third. For the time being, it felt okay.

After a few minutes I began to wonder whether I'd completely imagined what had happened in

Ruislip. My head told me not to get carried away, that this was only a gentle knock-up, not a competitive match. Yet inwardly I was positively beaming. Having Paul on the opposite side of the net had a lot to do with that. A few years ago someone in Hollywood invented a game called 'The Six Degrees of Kevin Bacon', the idea being that every actor or actress can in some way be connected to the star of *A Few Good Men* and *Apollo 13* within six moves. Take Harvey Keitel for example. Harvey was in *Reservoir Dogs* with Chris Penn, who had starred in *Footloose* with Kevin Bacon. A score of two. In my head I'd just invented a tennis equivalent. Here I was hitting with Paul Delgado, brother of Jamie Delgado, who had lost at Wimbledon the previous year to Andre Agassi. A score of three linking me to one of the greatest players of the modern era. YEAH BABY!

As we walked off court, Paul asked how the elbow felt. The answer was it felt fine. I hadn't hit the ball that hard, or taken a serve, but I seemed fit to continue. I thanked him for his time and walked back to the car.

"Remember! There's nothing to stop it coming back this afternoon, or tomorrow morning, or the day after that."

– "Piss off, John. I'm carrying on."

"Fine. Your decision. Just don't come moaning to me when the shit hits the fan. And it's MR McEnroe, you little prick."

I drove north-west from High Wycombe up the A40 towards Oxford, Vince's '*Music To Smash Heads By*' tape on the stereo to psyche me up again following the best part of a two-day lay-off. After Stokenchurch I came to a crossroads. Taking care to avoid the slip roads to the M40 motorway, I turned left and drove for several miles until I lost my bearings completely. Stopping to look at a map for the first time since leaving Warnham, I realised to my horror that I was now heading south-west towards the Berkshire Downs where, if the atlas was anything to go by, I'd have trouble finding roads let alone tennis courts.

On I went, past field after field of corn, searching for any kind of right turn that might put me back on track. Another quick glance at the map revealed I was now further south than High Wycombe. Bloody great. My best option seemed to be to carry on until I reached a place called Benson, just off the main route from Reading to Oxford. A few more turns in the road and I was there, standing beside the padlocked gates to the village tennis club. Four courts, good condition, all floodlit, but nobody around to play against. I decided to go and look for somewhere to spend the night, then return in search of a victim.

Fifty pounds seemed like a lot to spend on a room at a pub in an off-the-beaten-track Oxfordshire village, but sod it. I was a finely tuned athlete in need of some pampering, and deserved it.

Anyway, I'd played on smaller football pitches than Room Four at The Crown Inn, and the bar downstairs could always supply me with ice should the elbow start playing up again.

That evening I walked back to the tennis club and was amazed to discover at least 40 people either playing or awaiting their turn. I introduced myself to a dead ringer for Al Jardine out of The Beach Boys, who seemed to be organising some kind of rota. His name was Glynn Leaney, a nice fella who would repeatedly called me Ben over the next couple of hours. He proudly told me that Benson Tennis Club boasted over 200 members, including a thriving junior section. With a population around the 700 mark, I found this hard to believe until Glynn pointed out that many people drove from as far away as Reading just to play here. But why?

"Because we're friendly, perhaps a bit warmer than some other clubs in the area. You could be an axe-murderer for all I know, but we've welcomed you with open arms, haven't we?"

Fair point.

Glynn paired me up with a woman, whose name I immediately forgot, for a doubles match. We won the toss and somehow I ended up serving first. I decide to go for position rather than power, in other words simply to try and get the ball in. Expecting the lower half of my right arm to come shooting off at any moment, I served the first ball.

No sign whatsoever of the dreaded jelly elbow. And we won the point. Four serves later, we'd won the game. I felt like cracking open the champagne right there, lying down on the court in the evening sun and getting plastered.

What's-her-name and I took the set 6–4, during which I had to serve on two more occasions. Again no complaints. With so many people waiting to play, I took a break before risking a second set of doubles later, during which I felt confident enough to try a few more volleys and overhead smashes.

Afterwards I was hoping a few of the players would be up for a pint or two. Benson seemed to boast several pubs, and in something of a buoyant mood I was eager to check them out. But if there's one thing I do know about tennis clubs in England (besides the oft-quoted elitist tag), it's that they're not big on drink. Which is a shame, as I am. With the vast majority of sport played at an amateur level in Britain – from football to squash, golf to cricket – the visit to the bar after a match is mandatory. Not so tennis.

Benson Tennis Club proved to be no exception. Everyone had to go home to either put their kids to bed, get a good night's sleep for work the next day or indulge in a little wife-swapping with other Home Counties couples. All right, I made the last one up. But you get the point. So Billy No Mates made his way back to The Crown Inn for a couple of pints on his own, relieved that the elbow was still in one piece but wishing tennis clubs would every now and again behave like their rugby counterparts. You know, a tough five-setter followed by six hours on the Guinness, rude songs about what Steffi Graf can do with her nose, and seeing who can pee the furthest off a baseline. Then again, perhaps not.

CHAPTER SIX

Oxford

"Mike (Barson) had the bright idea of calling
us Morris & The Minors, and no-one dared
argue with him as he owned the Morris
van that we used. However, one day, while
discussing this sad name, someone said
'Let's pick a song from the set.' I replied,
'Oh yeah, like Madness. And the rest, as
they say..."

Graham McPherson, aka Suggs

Tuesday May 7th 2002 will go down as a bad day
in the Henman family. In Rome, young Tim crashed
out of the Italian Open in the first round while
suffering from a 'stomach virus' – the sporting term
for 'the shits'. Thirteen-hundred miles away in
Oxford, someone had overdone it at lunchtime and
thrown up on the pavement outside the family
solicitors run by Tim's parents, Tony and Jane. Two
thin streams had broken away from the main pool
of lager-induced vomit, doing their best to soil the

shoes of unsuspecting evening commuters running
for buses on St Aldate's.

A friend had warned me to expect to find plenty
of tennis courts in Oxford, both in public parks and
on land owned by the city's many colleges. So
I decided to do here what I'd done in West London
– park the Morris and go on foot. But not before I'd
taken her on a quick sightseeing trip first.

It was in February 1969, two months before
I was born, that RAA 954G rolled off the assembly
line at Morris Motors Limited in the Oxford
suburb of Cowley. To my knowledge, she hadn't
been back to the city since. I'd bought her in 1994,
the log book showing one previous owner who had
rarely left South Wales. On a journey that began
with me revisiting my childhood, I felt it was only
right the Morris should see where she came from.

The plant was impossible to miss, a maze of
factories running parallel to the Oxford ring road
for about a mile. It's now owned by BMW, and is
where the modern version of the Mini is made.
I swung the Morris round and parked her in a
lay-by outside the main gates.

"This is where you came from, darling. You and
thousands of others like you. Thirty-three years and
120,264 miles ago."

Silence.

"Of course you won't recognise it. You were too
young to remember. It's probably changed a bit
since then, and there wouldn't have been all these

German flags flying outside. But this is it. Cowley. Home of the Morris Minor."

RAA 954G was the fifth Morris Minor to enter the Vignes family. The first arrived in 1974 when my father finally got round to passing his driving test. He named it 'Sandra' after the wife of the previous owner, setting a precedent for all the others that followed. I learned to drive and took my test in 'Margaret', the car I inherited as a teenager and drove for five years until she suffered the auto equivalent of a broken back – a fractured crossmember. I was devastated.

RAA 954G has never had a proper name. The previous owner didn't have a wife, and there was no way she was ever going to have a sex change and become 'Alan'. So instead she has always been 'Moggie', or plain 'Mogs'. I bought her at a time when most people I knew were busy test-driving Mondeos, Montegos and the like. If I'm honest, it made no sense whatsoever getting another Morris. I was living in the Thames Valley, clocking up high mileages working for a newspaper, with friends dotted all over the country and family in Wales. So having a Morris wasn't exactly practical. But I let my heart rule my head, and paid £2,000 for her. In her first four years with me, 'Mogs' travelled further than she had during the previous twenty-five. Yet she has rarely let me down, though her workload is now shared with a boring but handy modern estate car.

Whisper it, but there has been the odd fleeting moment when I've thought about selling her, only to feel deeply ashamed afterwards. I've been driving Morris Minors since I was 17, and somehow turning my back on them now would be like selling my soul. Or throwing out my old Clash LPs. Just unthinkable.

I'd like to think she enjoyed her return to Cowley, and getting the opportunity to show the Germans what a real car looks like. I took a couple of pictures to record the moment, then drove into the city and parked her outside my cousin Jan's house for safekeeping.

My friend was certainly right about Oxford and tennis courts. On a walk that started in Abingdon Road to the south of the city centre, finishing four hours later in the University Parks, I counted 72 of them in eight different locations, 41 of which were grass. Incredibly, only one was being used, a court at New College where I met a French student by the name of Jeremy and his South Korean (the sport must be catching on over there) female friend called Sohee.

I knocked with Jeremy first, who handed over to Sohee after a couple of rallies. Both in their early twenties, I'd presumed they were tennis partners rather than an item. However, the longer Sohee hit with me, the more agitated Jeremy became. He was definitely getting jealous. "One more," she kept shouting after each ball had gone dead, and he would respond by either pulling a sulky face or making a loud tutting sound. Eventually he decided he'd had enough.

"You go now!" he said pacing towards me, his little Gallic chest puffed out in case I hadn't got the message. So I went, before I was tempted to wrap my Donnay around his pretty French head.

I came across six other colleges with courts, and on five occasions found someone willing to hit a ball with me. The fact that all five were the groundsmen employed to maintain them doesn't say much for the tennis-playing student population of Oxford. If indeed there is one. I asked Ian, the man employed to maintain the sports facilities shared by Hertford, Exeter and St Peter's Colleges, why the courts were so deserted.

"Well, I could say it's because there are exams coming up, but to tell you the truth these haven't been used in weeks."

I went to thank him for the quick game, but his anti-student rant had only just begun.

"There are meant to be matches here tomorrow, that's if anyone can be bothered to turn up. When they win, these are good courts. When they lose, they moan about how bad they are, how the surface isn't flat enough, all that kind of stuff. But I don't care. It all goes in one ear and out the other. I don't reckon they [the players] are any good anyway."

And that seemed to be the common consensus among each groundsman that I met. As one of them put it, "Exams or no exams, it doesn't seem to stop them all playing cricket."

I felt sure my luck would change in the University Parks to the north of the city, home to a dozen beautifully-manicured grass courts that looked as though they'd never been stepped on. I set the stopwatch running and sat down on a park bench, waiting for potential victims to walk by. Seven people turned down my offer of a quick rally. *Seven!* That's more refusals in 20 minutes than I'd had in the previous 12 days put together. Miserable gits.

Time up, I took a racket and ball and walked onto the nearest court to fire off one serve. Then I saw it. A dead grey squirrel, lying in the sun with its paws in the air just the other side of the net, eyes still open. I crouched down to take a closer look, just to make sure it wasn't playing games with me. A gentle poke with the racket confirmed my suspicions – one bona fide, stiff as a post, ex squirrel.

I decided to do the post-mortem myself. The two most common causes of squirrel death – motor vehicles and falling from great heights – were non-starters, with no roads in sight and the nearest tree a good 100 yards away. Which left either death through old age or by tennis player. You laugh, but many a little creature has met its maker by straying too close to a tennis court. The French player Michael Llorda killed a swallow outright with a powerful forehand shot during a doubles game at the 2002 Australian Open. And a few years ago in Indonesia, I played in a night match where my opponent connected with a low-flying bat instead of the ball while serving. It ended up dead in the net, he ended up too upset to carry on.

I've always liked squirrels, so I decided to give this one a proper send off – providing your idea of a proper send off is being manoeuvred onto the strings of a tennis racket, then tossed into some long grass. In the middle of this simple, moving ceremony, one of the Miserable Gits walked by again a few feet away. Keen to avoid eye contact, she didn't spot the furry bundle draped across the end of my racket. The schoolboy in me thought about lobbing it in her general direction, as pay-back for refusing to have a rally. But then she'd probably go to the police, and I'd be charged with breaking some ancient English law (punishable by hanging) forbidding the throwing of dead squirrels at pretty young female students.

Perhaps Oxford's empty courts were a blessing in disguise. The last thing I needed was plenty of fit young *Chariots of Fire* types challenging me to five-set duels. My elbow still felt okay, but I knew that whatever the problem had been, it could easily flare up again if put under too much pressure.

I broke sweat only once all afternoon. And it didn't happen on a tennis court. While walking across the running track at the Oxford University Sports Complex, having just enjoyed a quick rally with Groundsman Number Two, it suddenly dawned on me where I was. I'd stumbled on Iffley Road, scene of Roger Bannister's historic four-minute mile run in May 1954. Overcome by a sense of history, I dumped my bag by the side of the track, set my stopwatch running and ran for what I estimated was a mile, but was probably nothing like it. And recorded an earth-shattering time of six minutes, nine seconds. Not bad considering a stiff headwind and 15 years of beer, wines and spirits.

That evening Jan and her boyfriend Lloyd took me to their tennis club in an area called Hinksey, just outside the city. Having yet to hit a ball in anger all day, I felt ready for a serious challenge. And judging by his fighting pre-match talk, so did Lloyd. Apparently somebody had told him I used to be quite handy at this sport. As a result, he was out to get me.

Occasionally, when a professional tennis player is interviewed after winning a match, you might hear them say something like...

"The ball was as big as a house out there today."

Expressions like that have baffled many an armchair fan down the years. After all, how are you supposed to fend off a fast travelling, four-bedroom semi using only an egg-shaped frame and some strings? What the player means is that he or she could see the ball clearly, almost as soon as it left the other person's racket, and had time to position themselves ready to return the shot with attitude. In other words, they felt at the peak of their game.

In the 40-odd miserable minutes it took Lloyd to wipe the floor with me, I was seeing a ball the size of a sparrow's testicle. Despite feeling really positive beforehand, I just couldn't get going. My leg muscles felt 83 rather than 33 years old, whereas Lloyd was dancing round like the Patron Saint of Spring Chickens. I lost 6–0 6–2, the only bonus being that my elbow lasted the course.

"That's because you barely touched the ball," joked a smug Lloyd afterwards over a pint or four in The Wheatsheaf, the pub where Bill Clinton played saxophone during his Oxford under-graduate years. He was right though, and I was at a complete loss to explain my non-performance. Jan didn't help matters by saying she had expected "a bit more [from me] than that". Thanks, cousin.

I don't know which one of us suggested I should drive out to Weston-on-the-Green the following day. But, as ideas go, it was a bloody good one. Weston, to the north-east of the city, is the village Tim Henman grew up in, and where his parents still live. You've probably seen Mr and Mrs Henman on TV, sitting stone-faced in the players' balcony on Wimbledon's Centre Court, looking for all the world like they're at a funeral – even when their boy is on the verge of winning a match.

So the next morning the Morris and I went off in search of tennis courts in Weston. And in true Henmanesque tradition, it lashed down. So hard that at times the one-speed windscreen wipers on the car couldn't cope, and I had to pull over to avoid careering into the oncoming traffic. Peering through the Morris's rain-streaked windows, Weston didn't appear to have any rain-stops-play facilities for passing tennis players, not even a coffee shop. I asked one soggy local if there were any courts in the village, and he pointed me in the direction of the extremely plush Weston Manor Hotel, where apparently I would find the only one. If nothing else, I could at least wait there until the rain eased off.

I parked the Morris beside a gleaming AC Cobra, went inside, did my spiel to the receptionist on duty, who looked at me like she'd just come face to face with a Martian.

She panicked. "I'll get the manager."

The manager arrived, a Welshman called Neil John, and I repeated the spiel.

"Good gracious! I'd love to help you. Absolutely love to. But the court doesn't belong to the hotel, it belongs to the Henman family. They live right behind us."

YOU BEAUTY!

I asked if he could pull any strings to help me hit one serve on the hallowed Henman ground.

"I don't know. We've had some problems with hotel guests mistakenly thinking the court is ours and going over to use it. The last time it happened, Mrs Henman came out in her nightie to chase them off. Mr Henman does sometimes come over to use our swimming pool, so they might let you play. Why don't you go and ask them?"

And risk being confronted by Tim's mother in her nightie? *You cannot be serious!* But I'd come this far. I took a couple of deep breaths and walked down the overgrown track linking the hotel with the Henmans' place. Eventually I came to a house that looked like something you'd find in the pages of *Homes And Gardens*. It had to be theirs. I went up the garden path, tip-toed round some patio furniture and knocked on the back door. After a short wait a woman appeared, fully clothed, thank God. But then again it wasn't Mrs Henman.

I explained what the hell I was doing snooping around the family home of Britain's leading tennis player, in the rain, in my tennis kit. Then I asked who she was.

"I'm Mrs C, a friend of the family. That's all you need to know. No, I can't see any problem with you using the court. Go ahead."

I thanked her, and asked if she'd care to join me for a quick rally.

"I don't think so."

And before I could ask if Tim had recovered from the Rome shits, the door had closed.

I walked back across the garden surrounding the house, through an avenue of trees, into yet another large garden. And there it was. The court where little Timothy Henry Henman first started learning his trade aged two and a half, knocking up with his

97

parents and two elder brothers. This is going to sound like sour grapes, but if I'd been raised in surroundings like these then maybe I might have got a little further than village youth-club tennis finals and walk-on parts at county trials. Warnham had the odd posh touch, but this was another world. One beautifully-kept court beside a huge lawn with 'Marquee To Be Installed Here' written all over it. Dotted all around were benches taken from the old Court One at Wimbledon, knocked down in 1996, complete with little plaques vouching for their authenticity. I know you had to practise hard to get where you are Tim, but my God you had a head start, mate.

I selected the oldest, most beaten-up looking ball from my bag, knowing one serve in that weather would be the signature on its death certificate. Stupid to waste a new one. I wiped the rain from my brow so I could see properly, threw it into the air and hit it down the court. The surface was so wet the ball didn't even bounce, the poor thing leaving a trail of spray in its wake before coming to rest against the fence at the far end. And there it stayed, my very own personal calling-card to the Henman family.

In hindsight, I only wish I'd written a message on it, like the one I'd sent the All England Club. Something like 'Smile, Tony Henman. It won't hurt, honestly.' Then again, if people kept throwing up on the landing outside my office at home, I'd probably suffer a sense of humour bypass too.

CHAPTER SEVEN

Banbury Cross

"Tennis is a lonely sport. Most of the time you are travelling on your own."
Gabriela Sabatini

I've always believed that my mother and father were essentially good parents. Kind, loving, not afraid to give me a clip round the ear when I deserved it, and perhaps most importantly fun, or 'sparky' as Roald Dahl put it on the final page of *Danny The Champion of the World*. But over the years I've realised there is one embarrassingly large void in my life that I have to blame them for, especially now I'm on the verge of becoming a parent myself – I don't know any nursery rhymes.

As a child this wasn't really a problem, as our house was always full of music that I would sing along to. My parents had a good record collection, and I found that by the age of six I knew most of the words to *Rubber Soul*, The Beach Boys'

20 Golden Greats and a fair chunk of the songs from various Monty Python albums. Which on reflection seems pretty cool. Why bother with Humpty Dumpty when you can have *Baby You Can Drive My Car*? But as an adult, this void is something I've become increasingly ashamed of. Take games like Trivial Pursuit for instance, where questions about nursery rhymes are thrown in simply to act as a warm-up.

"Come on! *Hickory Dickory Dock, the mouse ran up the clock. The clock struck* ...what time?"

"I'm sorry, it doesn't matter how many times you say it, I haven't got a clue. Quarter to five?"

Cue disbelieving stares.

It's also a problem when you visit certain places, like London Bridge or York. Names that I'm reliably informed have had rhymes written about them. I might know the bare bones, something about a bridge falling down, or a Duke, but after that – blank. Driving north through the perma-rain from Weston-on-the-Green towards Banbury, it was the same old story. This much I knew – a horse gets ridden to a cross to see a lady who may or may not be on another horse (or was it the lady that was being ridden, which might explain why she was cross?). But I couldn't tell you what happened next if my life depended on it.

By now the weather was so bad I was beginning to feel angry, convinced that some all-powerful, unseen force was out to deny me my right to a summer day and some tennis. I arrived in Banbury in serious need of somewhere to dry out, do a bit of hand-washing and catch up with my notes about the Henman Experience. My mood quickly worsened as I began to realise that besides a nursery rhyme, Banbury was also famous for something else – rude hoteliers. One, a man in his fifties, asked me to wait at reception while he finished talking to his financial advisor in the next room. I knew it was his financial advisor because for the next ten minutes, I had to listen to them talking tax-breaks through the open door. I bet Andre Agassi never has to put up with this crap when he's checking in to the Miami Sheraton.

"Any chance of a room now?" I asked, having read every tourist information leaflet in reception several times over.

"I'll be through in five minutes."

"Are you like this with all your guests?"

That threw him.

"...because if you are, I'm not surprised you need financial advice. For all you know, I could be from a national newspaper here to do a feature on what to do and where to stay in Banbury. Couldn't I?"

"Are you?"

"I'll leave you to work that out. I'm walking out of here right now, but bear that in mind the next time someone comes and stands in your reception."

That's one of the advantages of being six foot three, reasonably well built with very short hair.

When push comes to shove, you have the ability to reduce rude little fuckwits like him to jelly. But fancy working in the tourist trade and not knowing whether travel journalists go on assignment dressed in shorts, tennis shoes and waterproof training tops. As bright as Alaska in December, as my old Californian friend Mark is fond of saying.

Eventually I found a place in Oxford Road with a spare bed and a friendly manager. On the plus side, the room was in a converted attic with great views overlooking the town. On the minus, the rain was so heavy that there was no view to see. Pounding away on the roof, it sounded like Keith Moon when he loses it at the tail end of *My Generation*. To make matters worse, the ceiling was barely six feet high and my nose had suddenly turned into an uncontrollable snot factory. I walked into town and bought a box of tissues and some 'max-strength' anti-flu drinks, then returned to my attic. And went straight to bed.

It rained all evening. By midnight most of the tissues had gone, the incessant racket on the roof making sleep virtually impossible. I wanted to call Alex, but knew she wouldn't appreciate me phoning in the middle of the night, especially if all I was going to do was moan about the weather and a runny nose. At some point I must have dozed off. I awoke just before 7am, the TV still on with the sound turned down from the night before, Keith Moon continuing with his extended drum solo.

And I felt like shit.

I called reception and reserved the room for another night. The manager asked if I was feeling okay, and I told him what every man says when they get a heavy cold – that I had the flu. Forget tennis, exploring Banbury and learning the words to my first nursery rhyme. After breakfast, I was going to go back to bed, watch daytime TV and start reading a book I'd bought in Oxford about the Scottish comedian and actor Billy Connolly. My only consolation was knowing that at least the elbow was getting a rest.

On Channel Three, a woman the size of Bradford was confronting her husband about his lover in front of a studio audience. He kept insisting there was no lover, that she was making it all up. That was until the lover came on. The wife flew at her, claws out. Security intervened, and everyone sat down again. The lover started talking about the time the husband had proposed having a threesome with the wife. And then she came out with the pièce de résistance – she was pregnant with his baby. That did it. The wife jumped up again, security dashed in to save the lover from a good kicking, and the wife ran out in tears. A cameraman followed her, eager to catch the floods backstage. Meanwhile in the studio, the man was busy dumping the lover, baby or no baby. She started crying. The whole thing was a complete car wreck. I didn't want to look but couldn't resist turning my head to take in the carnage.

Programme over, I boiled some water in the kettle beside my bed, poured myself another Max-strength, and flicked through the other channels. Two DIY shows, an Oprah repeat and a snowstorm where Channel Five should have been. Tennis players often moan about how their lives become nothing more than a merry-go-round of hotel rooms, aeroplanes and matches. Now, for the first time in my life, I could see where some of them were coming from. Okay, at least the cream of the crop could afford better accommodation than this, with room service and the latest DVDs to fend off the constant bombardment of home makeover programmes. And should they feel poorly, personal trainers are always at hand to make everything better again. But think about the other hundreds of unknowns struggling round the planet, trying to win enough matches to qualify for the bigger tournaments, picking up barely enough prize money to cover their expenses. What happens when they get a dose of the flu (sorry, heavy cold) or the dreaded Delhi Belly? It's bad enough falling ill in Banbury, but imagine if it happened in Bangalore, where a couple of phone calls home to your doctor would wipe out every penny you were due to earn that week. Not fun.

Still the rain fell, only now more Ringo Starr than Keith Moon, soothing enough to send me back to sleep. When I came to, the Six O'Clock News was on and the sheets were soaked with sweat. I opened a couple of windows (so the unfortunate soul assigned to cleaning the room wouldn't think someone had died in there), went for a shower and ordered a pizza from the local delivery shop. Which ended up being about the size of a two pound coin. And I still couldn't eat all of it. After 30 pages of Billy Connolly, a phone call to Alex ("Are you turning into a hypochondriac?") and another flu drink, I transferred to the other single bed in my room and fell asleep again.

Twelve hours later I had yet more sweaty sheets on my hands, but felt a lot better. Not fantastic, but well enough to hit a serve or two. I packed my bags, settled the bill for my room (which probably didn't even cover the laundry costs) and got back in the Morris. Stuff Banbury and any hope of learning the words to my first proper nursery rhyme. I'd do a quick tour round a few back streets in search of the odd court, then leave.

The People's Park sounded like the kind of place you'd expect to find in Moscow, not Oxfordshire, with a big statue of Lenin standing at the gates. With the rain on hold, the entire population of west Banbury seemed to have gone there, desperate to take in some fresh air before The Viking God Of Making It Rain Directly Over RAA 954G came back from his lunch break. And out of them all, I had to choose the Angry Young Man to play on the public courts.

My knock-up with Gary (late-teens, centre-parting, Limp Bizkit sweatshirt with hood) started fine. After a couple of rallies I suggested a short best-of-three-games match, keen not to overdo it after my bedridden day. Gary accepted. I won the first game, which he didn't seem to mind. But at the beginning of the second, with him serving, his mood suddenly changed. After a second double fault, he picked up a loose ball and hit it clean out of the park, across the road and into a garden.

Now balls aren't cheap, so that probably cost me around £1.30. I thought about saying something, then decided against it. Perhaps he was having problems at home, parents splitting up, dog had just died, that sort of thing. But then he did it again, after running for and failing to reach a drop shot.

"Er, do you mind? Those things aren't cheap."

"Fuck off!"

"YOU FUCK OFF!"

So he did. I suppose it could have been worse. When he threw the racket that I'd lent him, he did so sideways across the court rather than directly into the ground, which would undoubtedly have broken the frame. And if that had happened I'd have probably hit him, he'd have called the police, Banbury Magistrates would have sent me to an open prison somewhere in the middle of England, where I would have received death threats from his family. Which would have made a great story for this book, but not done my self-esteem (or marriage) any favours.

I drove north along the A423, unsure about where I was heading but just glad to see the back of Banbury. After a few miles I spotted a signpost for Leamington Spa. A couple of years ago, I'd read an article that mentioned a tenuous claim the town had to being the home of lawn tennis. Uncertain whether I'd be coming this way, I had dug it out from an old pile of newspaper cuttings and brought it along with me, just in case.

Leamington's claim went like this. Harry Gem, a solicitor, and Augurio Perera, a Spanish merchant, were mates who first met while working in Birmingham during the 1850s. Both were keen athletes who regularly played rackets, cricket and croquet, never the most strenuous of pastimes but still, nevertheless, sports. One afternoon they started experimenting with a new game in Perera's back garden in Edgbaston. They called it 'pelota', after the Basque game of the same name where players hit a ball with their hands using gloves. Pelota would eventually become lawn tennis, so if it hadn't been for Gem or Perera there would be no Wimbledon, Tim Henman would probably be working as a solicitor for his father's firm, I wouldn't have made this trip and you would now be reading something completely different. Maybe a book about me trying to play my way across England's croquet lawns without dying of boredom.

Anyway, back to the story. In 1872, both men decided to buy houses in Leamington, then an extremely fashionable spa town that attracted people from across the whole country, including Queen Victoria. There they met two doctors called Frederic Haynes and Arthur Tomkins and introduced them to their new game. That summer the four men formed the world's first lawn tennis club, Gem being elected as president. They played in the gardens of Leamington's prestigious Manor House Hotel beside the River Leam, using white balls and courts marked out by cords or white tape fastened down with pins. For many years afterwards the hotel hosted an annual tennis tournament, organised by the Leamington Lawn Tennis Club. Gem apparently even wrote a tune called *The Wearing of the Green* to mark the close of the season in October 1874, in which he described players as 'pelota boys'. Mercifully, no living soul appears to know how it goes.

And then everyone promptly forgot about the four of them and their rightful place in tennis history. There is no record of Haynes, who lived until 1935, being invited to the celebrations marking the 50th anniversary of the Wimbledon Championships in 1926, while neither the late Gem, Perera or Tomkins got a mention in the official book published to mark the event. And I thought I had grounds for being browned off at the All England Club.

Then, in 1969, someone came across a collection of papers that Harry Gem's widow had presented to the Birmingham Reference Library shortly after her husband's death. Among the papers were the rules of the Leamington Lawn Tennis Club, drawn up in 1874, which includes some of the following gems:

- payment of an annual subscription of half a guinea
- each court to be 30 yards long by 12 yards wide, divided into right and left hand courts, with reduced dimensions for women
- the net should be four feet high
- payment of a shilling to club funds on losing a game to love (can you imagine the All England Club trying to introduce that one now!)
- a fine of one shilling on losing a ball.

After that everyone wanted a piece of the Harry Gem & Co bandwagon. In 1972 the Lawn Tennis Association, together with Leamington Spa Council, organised a big shindig at the Manor House Hotel to mark the centenary of the founding of the world's first lawn tennis club, and matches were staged in period costume dress in the gardens.

With all that in mind, there was only really one place I could stay in Leamington, providing the Manor House hadn't been knocked down since 1972 and had a room for less than £80, my self-imposed limit when it came to overnight stops. Driving down the town's impossibly white, open-terraced streets, I discovered it almost by accident, an impressive red-brick building shaded from the road by a huge oak tree. I parked the Morris and went in.

"Hi there. Can you tell me, this is the Manor House Hotel famous for being home to the world's first-ever lawn tennis club, isn't it?"

Judging by the irritated look on the receptionist's face, I wasn't the first tennis groupie to have come in search of the game's 'spiritual home'. I was, however, probably the first to do so wearing tennis gear, which could be construed as taking an interest a little too far. Like those freaks who turn up at Wimbledon pretending to be players, parading around the outside courts dressed head to toe in Nike carrying a bag of rackets over one shoulder. Yes, it really happens.

I explained why I was there, which seemed to calm her nerves, and she began sifting through the hotel register.

"All our rooms are full at the moment, but we do have one round the back in a separate block which is used for staff accommodation. Will that do? I could do you a discount?"

Lovely-jubbly.

The block, together with a car park, had been built on land sandwiched between the rear of the hotel and the river, on top of the gardens where Gem and the 'pelota boys' had played. After unloading the car, I pulled out a racket and started hitting a ball against a wall on the spot where it all began, as a kind of tribute. Lost in the moment, I didn't spot the huge tourist coach waiting for me to let it through, at least not until I lost control of the ball which smacked into the driver's wing mirror. How not to make friends and influence people.

Later that afternoon I called my friend Ralph, another Sussex exile now living north of Watford, to see if he fancied a quick tennis match while I was in town.

"God I'd love to, but I've got the flu. You don't sound too bright either."

"No, I've been struggling for the last couple of days but I'm feeling a lot better now. How about a pint and a curry instead?"

"Excellent! It's probably easier if I come to you. Meet you in the hotel bar about seven and we'll go from there."

Everyone has someone in his or her life that swings dangerously close to being Rob Gordon, the vinyl-loving list-maker from Nick Hornby's *High Fidelity*. Ralph Harrison is my Rob Gordon. Except Ralph is heavily into sport as well as music, which makes him twice as bad as Rob. So at some point during our get-togethers I know I'm going to be bowled something like this:

"Right – top three goals scored from outside the penalty area by Brighton & Hove Albion players with moustaches during the 1978/79 season?"

Which is easy, as we're both big Brighton fans, or:

"Top five blondes from the 1983 Ladies Singles Championship at Wimbledon."

Which I'd probably struggle with after the goddesses that were Carling Bassett and Andrea Temesvari – oh, and maybe Sue Barker.

Ralph is great company even with the flu, and especially after two nights holed up in a germ-filled attic in Banbury. Instead of hitting his adopted town, we decided to stay put in the hotel lounge and order some food from the hotel kitchens. Halfway through my first chicken fajita, I decided to play Ralph at his own game by asking for three Leamington claims to fame.

"Well there's this place for a start, birthplace of lawn tennis."

"How did you know that?"

"Because you told me, but I think I knew about it anyway. Then you've got the spa waters and the fact that a lot of Coventry City players live in the area. But this thing about Leamington being where tennis all began is fascinating. They should make more of that round here. I bet if you went into town and asked ten people what Leamington is famous for, none of them would say that."

So the next morning, after shaking off the mind-numbing effect of several pints of Boddingtons mixed with a medicinal drink (that'll teach me to read the warning labels on those things), that's exactly what I did – went up to ten people out walking along The Parade and asked each one for a reason why Leamington was famous. Once I'd stopped feeling like some daytime TV presenter doing a washing powder advert, I quite enjoyed it. Here are the results:

6 – said the spa waters

2 – said Queen Victoria

1 – said its parks and open-spaces

And the remaining one, a middle-aged guy with a passing resemblance to the comedian Paul Merton, said the railway station. I was so stunned I asked him to repeat it in case I'd misheard him.

"The railway station. It's not really famous, I know, but I like the building. That okay?"

Fine by me. Nobody said tennis, which I found sad but not entirely surprising. If there are any sporting entrepreneurs out there, then here's an idea for you. Buy the Manor House Hotel, turn it into a tennis museum, bulldoze the accommodation block where I stayed, and relay the lawns and old fashioned courts where Gem and his cronies used to play. A sure-fire tourist hit if ever there was one. You could even get Carling Bassett or Andrea Temesvari to do the opening ceremony. I'll add it to *my* list of things to do when I win the lottery.

Survey completed, I went for a stroll around Leamington's green spots, starting with Top Park, home to four tennis courts. None were being used, so I set the stopwatch and waited for someone to walk by. That someone proved to be Tim Moore, who said he was a salesman. Dressed in an expensive black suit and what I think were Gucci shoes, he agreed to a quick rally. Our knock lasted three hits, probably the shortest of my trip so far. Then again if I wore shoes costing somewhere in the three-figure region, I wouldn't risk scuffing them on a tennis court. He suggested I head in the direction of Victoria Park, where I would find "plenty of courts and people to play against".

Tim was right about the courts, wrong about the people. I waited 20 minutes during which not a single player turned up. Two passing dog-walkers also turned down my advances (though one terrier, given hands and a more tolerant owner, would definitely have been game for a set). Time up, I took a serve and returned to the Manor House Hotel to pack the Morris and check out.

Back behind the wheel, I cruised twice around Leamington's one-way system, desperate not to make the same mistake I'd made after High Wycombe by heading south. I knew Birmingham wasn't too far away, despite what the road signs were trying to tell me. Kenilworth, Coventry, Rugby, Solihull, but no Brum whatsoever. Perhaps Warwickshire County Council had some kind of problem with Britain's second largest city, like the local accent or the fact it gave us Duran Duran.

I chose the Kenilworth road, but then the signs let me down altogether by disappearing completely.

After a few miles of fields punctured by the odd mini-roundabout, I came to a village called Knowle and immediately spotted a court in a garden. Signal, brake, just miss cat on a grass verge, stop, walk back, say hello to woman pruning roses, do spiel.

Her name was Anne Duffy. Her husband was a civil engineer who had built the court for their children, only now they'd dumped tennis for skateboarding, which explained the ramps on the gravel surface where a net once stood. Over a cup of tea, I told her all about my trips; she kept apologising for the state of the court, in the way people do when guests arrive unannounced and the house is in a mess.

"We really ought to do something about it, but it's just finding the time. We love having it there. It's just never used for tennis anymore. Perhaps if we patched it up, then we'd start playing again."

Maybe they would, but Anne still declined my offer of a knock, opting instead to watch me hitting one serve between the skateboard ramps. I thanked her for the tea and she accompanied me back down the garden path. As we parted, I asked her which direction I was heading in.

"You're going towards Birmingham. You'll get to Solihull first, but that's Birmingham by everything but name. You can't miss it. Best of luck now."

CHAPTER EIGHT

Parents

"The baggage that came along with this girl was excessive. We needed a van for it."
Tennis coach Nick Bollettieri on his former protegée
Monique Viele – and her parents

The terminal blow that killed Michael Costin was said to have been so hard, it almost severed his head from his body. The 40-year-old father of four had been watching his son take part in an ice hockey practice-match in Cambridge, Massachusetts, when he became involved in an argument with 19-stone truck driver Thomas Junta, whose boy was playing in the same game. The argument, initially over alleged rough play, ended up with Costin's head being repeatedly slammed against the floor in front of a dozen hysterical children. Afterwards, Junta calmly walked out of the ice arena and drove home, where he was arrested by police.

Think it could only happen in America? In January 2002, a child playing in a football match in

Sussex was punched in the face by an adult spectator, simply for daring to tackle an opponent. Thankfully the victim wasn't seriously hurt. In Maroubra, New South Wales, one irate dad held a cricket umpire by the scruff of the neck after he gave his son out, refusing to let go until he changed his decision.

Stateside, this growing trend has even been given a name – 'sideline rage' – the morphing of normally calm, rational parents into Grade A nutters at the slightest glimpse of a puck or soccer ball.

Strange days indeed, as John Lennon once sang. Yet anyone who has followed tennis down the years will be accustomed to barking-mad parental behaviour, albeit of a verbal rather than a physical nature. Damir Dokic, father of Jelena, once got drunk at Wimbledon, wrapped himself in a Union Jack, slagged England off as a fascist state and smashed a journalist's mobile phone. Mary Pierce of France broke all ties with her pa for continually shouting insults at her and her opponents during matches.

In a nutshell, tennis parents are nightmares, the kind of people who will not rest until little Freddie or India makes the world number one spot.

Moving house, changing citizenship, pawning their kidneys, whatever helps the cause. All too often, it ends in tears, with the child burnt out and hating the game by their mid-teens, cursing their parents for depriving them of a normal childhood.

Those that do make it as professionals, particularly the girls, often end up clashing with mum or dad over prize money, boyfriends, training schedules, nights out with friends and, for the pretty ones, fashion shoots. Eventually, as Martina Hingis once put it, the youngster wants "more space and independence".

To the east of Solihull town centre, I came across a tennis club where two young girls were playing a match against each other. Both were being watched from the sidelines by their fathers. The taller girl, with her elegant textbook strokes, had a game to die for. However, dad was proving to be something of a tougher opponent than her peer at the other end of the court. He just wouldn't stop haranguing her.

"Come on, Stephie, eye on the ball!"

"Stephie, what have I told you about staying on your toes?"

"Nice shot, Stephie. Let's have some more of that!"

"Bad choice, Stephie. What's wrong with using your backhand?"

Poor old Stephie was struggling to deal with this constant bombardment. On a couple of occasions, I caught her throwing evil glares in his direction. When a forehand volley landed out and father started off on yet another sermon, she cut him short by throwing her racket to the ground and letting fly with a shrill, piercing "Dad!". That seemed to do the trick for a few minutes, until Stephie foot-faulted on a second serve, and off he went again.

"What have I told you about standing further back when you serve? That's going to keep on happening until you start listening to me."

At which point I wanted to walk over, put a fist down his throat and rip out his voice box. Then give him a smack round the face for good measure.

My own father would have loved it if I had become a professional tennis player. He wanted me to win Wimbledon so I'd have enough cash to buy him a Mercedes convertible. Every year, come the last week in June, he would remind me about it. Of course, it was never going to happen – we both knew that. But the older I got, the more of a joke it became. When Boris Becker won the Championship in 1985 aged 17, I remember the TV cameras zooming in on his proud parents in the stands, at which point my father, adopting a wobbly German accent, said "To zee car showroom tomorrow, Boris, to buy your father zat Robin Reliant, ya?"

Well, it seemed funny to me at the time.

My father believed that above all, sport should be fun. Play competitively by all means, but do it with a smile on your face. He wasn't one of those parents who frog-marches their child onto a tennis court the moment it pops out of the mother's womb. You'll find no camcorder footage of yours truly, aged four, walloping balls past some poor bugger five times my age. And you know what? I'm glad. Because there's something unnatural about any parent who forces their child to play tennis for three hours every day before they've even reached school age.

I will be forever grateful to my father for not being a pushy parent, not trying to live his own frustrated sporting dreams through his child. I never won Wimbledon. He died without ever getting to sit behind the wheel of a Mercedes. But at least I have nothing but happy memories of what sport meant to the two of us – him ad libbing a song on the guitar in praise of my first goal for Warnham Bucks, watching Wales play rugby in Cardiff, trips to Wimbledon and a pint on the common afterwards – which is more than can be said for poor old Mary Pierce.

Stephie finished her match and trotted to the net to shake hands with her opponent. She'd played well, given the circumstances, and won convincingly. The father of the beaten girl clapped the two of them from the court. Ten feet to his right, Stephie's dad stood looking down at the floor, shaking his head.

The Robert de Niro in me wanted to go over and have a word, tell him how lucky he was to have a talented daughter like Stephie, that if he carried on like that he'd wake up one morning to find an empty space at the breakfast table. Instead I bit my tongue as they collected their gear, climbed into a Peugeot estate and drove away.

With the court and the club deserted, I took my one serve, then headed off in the direction of England's second city.

CHAPTER NINE

From Despair to Where?

> "Birmingham wasn't and isn't a very rich area. It was rather dreadful and everybody in my family worked in factories, really mindless jobs that were physically exhausting."
>
> Ozzy Osbourne

Day 17. Take away the elbow-enforced rest, the Banbury cold, plus a few hours here and there drinking in bars during the evenings, and that made it about 14 days spent in tennis shoes, shorts and tops. Which feels pretty weird on the skin when you're used to living in grubby old sweatshirts and jeans.

There's something perfectly acceptable about walking around places like Oxford, Leamington and Leatherhead in tennis clothes. And I'll tell you why. Here are the first three things that come into

my mind when I see someone dressed to play tennis
in Britain:

1 Oh look, there's a sporty kind of person who...
2 certainly isn't from a working-class background
    and...
3 looks like they might have a bit of cash to burn.

Oxford, Leamington and Leatherhead (not to
mention virtually everywhere else I'd visited so
far) are full of sporty people who aren't from
working-class backgrounds and have a bit of cash
to burn.

On the other hand, the Birmingham suburbs of
Ladywood, Five Ways and Winson Green are not.
Which makes me extremely stupid for even
thinking about walking through them in my tennis
gear. For once, I broke my golden rule when it
comes to travelling – do some research about the
place you are about to visit, and anywhere you
might have to pass through to get there. And I
would pay the price for doing so. Big time.

I had arrived in Birmingham's southern suburbs
the previous evening and found a friendly hotel to
stay at in Moseley called The Gables. That night I
sat in the bar and read the local papers over dinner.
The good news – Birmingham City Football Club
had been promoted to the Premier League, and the
players would be taking to the streets the following
day in an open-top bus to celebrate. The bad news
– Birmingham was in danger of losing its position
as Britain's lap-dancing capital, with one venue

having closed and two others stopping all erotic acts. So any City fans wanting to party after hours while ogling the finest chests in the West Midlands looked set to be disappointed.

Done with the papers, I borrowed a street map from reception. Birmingham City's good fortune spelled trouble for me, as the streets would be rammed with traffic, making getting anywhere impossible. So I decided that come the morning, I would leave the Morris at the hotel and walk again, as I'd done in London and Oxford. Judging by the map, I seemed to have three options – straight up through the city centre, north-west towards Handsworth or north-east in the direction of lots of railway lines. I've never once seen a tennis court sandwiched between Boots and W H Smiths, or beside any signal boxes for that matter, so north-west won by default.

That said, the opportunity to visit somewhere so socially, politically and culturally different to Dorking, or Putney, or Banbury, did sound appealing. And Handsworth was definitely that somewhere, tattooed into the national consciousness ever since the night in September 1985 when a policeman arrested a black motorist following a row over a parking ticket. The riot that followed led to two deaths, 75 police officers and 35 civilians being injured, 83 buildings being torched, 437 arrests and an £8 million bill for the damage. It also provoked 'copycat' riots over the following month in other areas of Birmingham, as well as Bristol, Brixton and Tottenham.

I'd heard that Handsworth had bounced back to become a bustling, thriving area full of colour and life. I had no idea whether I'd find any tennis courts there, but the map showed a few public parks, so I was optimistic. Looking back, I have no idea why I didn't check what areas I'd be walking through to get there from Moseley. I just went blundering off, carrying my bag of rackets and balls. Untouchable me, a seasoned round-the-world veteran, big and ugly enough to look after myself. I wish.

The walk started well enough. I discovered some courts in Moseley's Cannon Hill Park, where I made up the numbers in a doubles game involving two Marks and a Dave, all playing in jeans. Dave had been alone on one side of the net until I arrived, but together we put on a pretty good performance to win a set 6–3. If I knew then what I know now, I would have finished by lining all three up against a wall and firing a ball repeatedly at their groins. Because I told them what I was doing, and in which direction I was heading. Yet at no time did they say anything like "I wouldn't go there if I were you," or "Are you a sandwich short of a picnic, mate?" They just let me go on my way. Bastards.

The gut feeling that maybe I'd bitten off more than I could chew first surfaced near the city end of Pershore Road, not too far from Edgbaston Cricket Ground. No tennis courts, but plenty of derelict flats and houses, some of them burned out. But why panic when you're walking beside one of the main arteries into the city, in full view of the suits in their flash BMWs and Audis? Okay, so the clues were right there in the traffic – sunroofs shut, windows up, doors centrally locked, a marked reluctance to stop even for traffic lights – but I didn't twig. So on I went, across a dual carriageway into a high-rise estate (not a parked car to be seen, another clue missed) and into Ladywood.

By now the BMW drivers had disappeared, replaced by shady figures on street corners who all looked as though they'd been in early-eighties bands like The Specials or The Beat, only to fall on hard times since. In my fancy Reebok shoes, whiter than white shorts and blue training top, rackets jutting out of my rucksack like lightning conductors, I was beginning to attract attention. Throw in the shades and shaved head, and you were looking at a pretty accurate identikit of the missing seventh member of Village People – the Red Indian, the Biker, the Construction Worker, the GI, the Cop, the Cowboy *and the Tennis Player...* Small wonder a group of young mothers standing at a bus stop stopped talking when they saw me approaching, one of them bursting into fits of laughter and shaking her head as I walked by.

I stopped outside the sanctuary of Ladywood Police Station, beside the 'Wanted For Robbery' notice board, and had a look at my street map.

Handsworth looked fairly close, and as all the Guinness in Dublin wouldn't get me going back the way I'd come, I pressed on. It seemed I'd made the right decision when, within minutes, I came across three courts in Summerfield Park, just over the road from Winson Green Prison. So what if none of them had nets? I set the stopwatch and, heart somewhat in mouth considering the location, waited for the first passer-by.

"Game of tennis, mate?"

I looked up just in time to see a bare-chested guy with long unkempt hair crawling out from beneath a bush, closely followed by another man and a girl.

"I'm Agassi's son. Game of tennis?"

For reasons that will soon become apparent, I'm not going to mention this fellow's real name. But for the sake of it, let's call him Mick. Mick and his mates had gone into the bush to take drugs. He wouldn't say exactly what, but from his 100-mile-an-hour way of walking and talking, speed seemed a safe bet.

I handed him a racket and we began to hit over where a net had once stood. And considering he hadn't any shoes and was probably seeing 30 different balls all at the same time, he was remarkably good.

"Haven'tdonethisinages.   Greatgamethough. Usedtoplayitasakid. Wereyouwaitingforsomebody?"

"Pardon?"

Mick took the hint and repeated the last line a

touch slower. I began telling him about my trip, but he didn't seem interested and interrupted me almost as soon as I'd started speaking.

"I bet you can't hit her tin with a serve," he said excitedly, gesturing towards the girl and the can of Fosters lager she was holding. Within seconds he had wrenched it from her grasp, poured away its contents (receiving an almighty "FUCK OFF" from the girl for his efforts), run back onto the court and placed it inside one of the service boxes.

"Go on, hit it!"

At the third attempt, I did, and the thing went spinning into the air and landed with a crash further down the court.

"Fucking whheeeyyyyyyyyyy!!!" said Mick. "That's gotta deserve some of this." And off he ran towards his friends again.

Sensing trouble, I packed the rackets and balls away should a quick dash be necessary, and walked over to the spot of grass where the three of them were now all sitting cross-legged. The other guy was using an old camping stove to heat a piece of foil containing some kind of resin.

"I don't take that shit anymore," said Mick. "Went off it a long time ago. But you're welcome to have some."

Besides the odd spliff (strictly no inhaling, you understand), I've always classified myself as a bit of a drug dunce. However, I'd recently read an article about an ex-footballer who had fallen on hard times and taken to 'chasing the dragon', the process of heating heroin until it turns to oil, then breathing in the fumes. The footballer had died of his addiction, which led me to believe that accepting Mick's offer probably wouldn't be a good career move.

Standing over the three of them, watching the oil beginning to bubble, my whole body went cold. It was like a scene out of *Trainspotting*, the camera panning back to reveal a tennis player lying spread-eagled in the park with a needle sticking out of his arm, Lou Reed's *Perfect Day* playing over the top.

"Sorry Mick, I've gotta be in Handsworth to meet someone in half-an-hour," I lied. "Thanks for the game. You take care of yourself."

"You sure you don't want some?"

"I'm sure."

"Tell everybody you had your arse whipped by Agassi's son. Good, wasn't I?"

I nodded and left them to it.

By now it was early afternoon. Time for a spot of refreshment. I came to a pub called The Old Smithy, which looked okay from the outside give or take several hundred layers of dust kicked up by the passing traffic. I went in and knew immediately that I'd made a mistake. No music, no talk, just the sound of the barman washing glasses. The handful of drinkers scattered about the place didn't just look up as I walked to the bar, so much as physically turn their whole bodies round to watch me. I ordered a pint of bitter shandy and stood at the bar, eyes fixed straight ahead so as not to catch anyone's gaze. It took me barely five minutes to finish my drink, and the only word I heard spoken during that time was a "Thanks" from the barman after I handed him a fiver.

Emerging blinking back into the sunshine, I walked a few yards before stopping to take another look at the map, just to make sure I was heading in the right direction. And then I heard his voice.

"You a fookin poof or somethin', because you look like a fookin poof."

I spun round and came face to face with a dark-haired stocky guy who, from his opening line, also thought he'd stumbled across the seventh Village Person. He was only about five foot eight, but from the state of his nose I could tell he'd done this sort of introduction before. I hadn't spotted him inside the pub, but couldn't see where else he'd appeared from. And he stank of booze.

"I should fookin' hit you, you fagggrrrrrr," which I think translated as 'faggot', but couldn't be 100 per cent certain about. Swaying gently, he took a deep breath, then continued.

"...cause people like you... queers... shouldn't fookin' be arannnnnd here."

I honestly can't recall what I said in return, but it was something along the lines of not wanting any trouble, and why didn't he just go back inside the pub. I hoped my height, plus the fact I hadn't run

131

off in floods of tears, might make him think again. I prayed it would, because I knew that if it did kick off, he would make pancakes out of me. I was never exactly Muhammad Ali to start with, but since my football accident I had found it impossible to completely clench my right fist. Throwing one punch would probably cause what remained of the bone structure to shatter.

So there we were. Me, him, plenty of passing traffic, but nobody up close enough to hear what was going on and step in to help me.

And then the punch came. I dodged to my right and his fist caught me on the left shoulder instead of my face. Blame the alcohol, the fact he was hitting uphill, or my quick reaction, but his aim was well and truly out. Thank God.

Then I bluffed him in the deepest, toughest tone I could muster.

"Do that once more, and you *will* regret it. Okay?"

He paused. Perhaps he hadn't realised how pissed he was. The punch had had little effect on me physically (though obviously inside I was shitting myself). That seemed to have thrown him. He didn't know what to do. Which was a good thing, as neither did I.

A couple of seconds went by, which seemed to last a couple of hours. And then he said:

"ARRRRRR, FOOK OFF!!!!!!"

I turned and walked slowly away. Somehow I

knew he wouldn't be coming after me. Every remaining ounce of strength seemed to have gone into that final "Fook off!", causing him to visibly deflate in front of me, his upper body folding over until his hands came to rest on his knees. When I reached the bend in the road, I looked back. He was still there, only now sitting down on the pavement, his head tucked between his legs. It looked for all the world like he was crying.

I can't remember much about the remaining mile or so to Handsworth. My head was spinning. What next? I'd wanted something a bit different to Oxford, and I'd got it. The druggies may have been druggies, but at least they'd been friendly. Pub Fighter, however, had left a sour taste in my mouth. Plodding along, he was in danger of making me hate Birmingham and everything about it. Throughout the remainder of Day 17, I just didn't want to be there. I've been threatened plenty of times over the years by loonies while travelling abroad, and written it off as character-building stuff. When it happens somewhere like the West Midlands, it's just a little bit close to home.

Yet in the back of my mind, I knew the whole sorry affair had only come about because of what I was wearing. In modern Britain, just looking different is enough to make you a target. The people of Birmingham and the West Midlands – where blacks fight whites, whites fight Asians, Asians fight blacks, and so on – know that better than most. But the colour of my skin wasn't an issue here. Neither was my religion or whether I'd said anything offensive to provoke the assault. I'd been picked on for my *tennis whites*. Now I've heard of football fans being attacked for wearing their favourite team's colours into the wrong pub. But when you can't walk the streets in tennis clothes without fearing for your life, what hope has the game ever got of converting the inner-city masses?

Poor old Handsworth. Britney Spears could have been performing topless in the High Street and I don't think I'd have been in the mood to watch. Everywhere I walked, the music and the fashions were loud. People seemed to be genuinely friendly. When I passed a record shop and said "Hi" to the half-a-dozen guys in dreadlocks standing outside, each one greeted me in return. But while I could still feel the imprint of Pub Fighter's fist on my shoulder, I remained on edge.

Outside Handsworth Leisure Centre, around 50 kids were taking part in a 25-a-side football match on the remains of two tennis courts. In one corner, a black teenager was practising some basketball shots, hurling obscenities at the footballers every time their ball came near him. I sat on a grass bank and watched them all charge about for the best part of an hour. Once the football game had finished and the courts cleared, I walked over to challenge the basketball player to a rally.

"Get away from me as fast as possible, receding white man."

Well, he didn't actually say that. But his glare, which suggested I'd been responsible for every civil rights atrocity ever committed against anyone of African-Caribbean origin, certainly did. Message received, I took my racket and served one ball over yet another missing net, then went off to find the nearest bus stop to start the return journey back to Moseley.

Which in the end took almost as long as my walk through the Badlands. Birmingham City's footballers had succeeded in their mission to create traffic chaos. The open-top bus ride had finished over three hours earlier, yet still the streets were gridlocked. After staring at the same *Spiderman* billboard for half-an-hour, I abandoned the crowded single-decker and walked the rest of the way into the city centre. I headed up Great Charles Street, past the museum and art gallery in search of Paradise Street, where I'd been told my connecting bus to Moseley would depart from. When I got there a man armed with a walkie-talkie told me that because of all the traffic problems, the Moseley bus was trapped in Moseley. At that moment, I detested Birmingham more than I detested any other city in the world. I wanted some great big, Monty Pythonesque boot to come crashing down on top of it all. And if it took me out, then so be it – it would have been well worth the sacrifice. No wonder

135

Ozzy Osbourne, Toyah and that guy with the fuzzy hair out of the Electric Light Orchestra got out of here as soon as they could afford the train fare.

Back at the hotel, the manageress asked me how my day had gone. I couldn't be arsed to explain all the gory details, so I said it had gone fine.

"Good, good. When you said where you were going, we did worry a bit. You hear about all sorts of things happening in places like Ladywood. Rapes, murders, car-jackings. But you had a good day. Would you like some dinner?"

Thanks for the warning then. Thanks a million.

I didn't sleep much that night. And Pub Fighter was only partly to blame. Let's just say a guy called Gilbert in the room next door was given the time of his life by a woman who liked the sound of his name. At one point I thought the bed was about to come through the wall.

After breakfast I drove back to Handsworth to pick the up the trail from the night before, safe in the knowledge that nobody in their right mind would car-jack a Morris Minor. Heading east across the northern suburbs, I came to a place called Aston Hall, a huge red-bricked building on a hill sandwiched between the Aston Expressway and Villa Park football ground. I'd love to tell you a bit about its history, who put it there and why, but I can't as it was locked up and there wasn't an information board anywhere in sight. So if you're that fussed, look it up on the internet. What fascinated me were the gardens surrounding it. Acres of flower beds, tree-lined avenues and grassy open spaces that looked stunning, particularly on a beautiful morning like that with the sun beginning its steady climb into a clear blue sky.

Of course something had to let the place down. Four tennis courts, all vandalised beyond belief, no nets, the remains of two burnt out cars scattered across one of them. Lovely. I sat in the shade of an oak tree and waited for a passer-by to pounce on. In the distance, two kids were playing a one-on-one game of football, using jumpers for goalposts. The intensity of their match was incredible to watch, every blade of grass being fought over with sliding tackles, shoulder challenges and last-ditch goal line clearances. With nobody else about, I decided to walk over and ask them to have a hit with me. It was only when I got closer that I realised both were grown men in their mid-twenties.

Mohammed and his friend, also called Mohammed, were security guards, due to start 12-hour shifts at a local warehouse at lunchtime. They'd come here to pass the morning and keep fit ("Believe me. You get no exercise whatsoever doing what we do," said Mohammed Number One). I handed both of them rackets and the three of us began knocking a ball about on the one court that was still just about usable. Both seemed naturals, so I asked if either of them had considered taking up tennis as a way of working out.

"You've seen the state of these courts," said Mohammed Number Two. "How can you play a proper game of tennis on a court that hasn't got a net? There are some others near here, but they're not much better. And it costs a lot of money to hire a good one. A couple of years ago, some mates and I played on a court out near Sutton Coldfield, and it cost us six quid an hour. Six quid! Imagine if there was only two of you, and you played for three hours. How much is that?

"Eighteen quid, nine quid each," chipped in Mohammed Number One.

"That's right. Who can afford that? Playing football costs you nothing. You just put down some posts and start playing."

And no sooner had the words come out of his mouth than Mohammed Number Two tripped while running for a backhand, landing awkwardly and cutting the palm of his left hand on a piece of broken glass. Blood immediately started seeping out from what appeared to be a deep cut. I hurried back to the Morris to find the plasters I'd brought with me in case of blisters, and wrapped one over the affected area.

"I think it looks worse than it is," he said. "I'll be okay."

Game over, I offered him a lift to the nearest hospital to get the injury seen to properly. He declined. His shift began in just over an hour, and he didn't want to be late.

"I'm already on a warning. One more and they could fire me. Thanks though. Where are you going next?"

I had no idea. But Sutton Coldfield sounded good. The Mohammeds gave me some directions, which I immediately forgot, and we went our separate ways.

Sutton Coldfield – sounds like a Victorian private eye, but is in fact one of Birmingham's posher suburbs. Now the posher suburbs of any city tend to be littered with tennis courts, but I could find only one here, situated in a park with no name. And none of the six people I challenged fancied a quick game. Actually, that's not strictly true. A middle-aged man called Paul did, but he was partially sighted, and felt he wouldn't be up to it.

"Now if the ball had a bell in it, that would be a different matter," he said. "Put a bell in any ball – a football, a cricket ball, anything except maybe a rugby ball – and a blind or partially-sighted person will be able to follow it and take part in that sport. But you could hit ten serves at me now, and I wouldn't get any of them back. Not a hope. Sorry."

I walked with Paul and his guide dog, Bess, into Sutton town centre, where we had a chat over a coffee. I told him about my trip, and he talked about his career as an electrician, one he'd been forced to give up in his mid-forties due to failing eyesight brought on by diabetes.

"I tell you what. Not being able to see has actually made me appreciate life a lot more. Sure, there are a lot of things I can't do now that I used to. I'd love to be able to play tennis with you, or go and watch the Villa (Aston Villa). But I've developed other interests to replace them, like going to concerts. When I used to go and see bands, I'd spend the whole time looking at the lights, the musicians, the crowd and whatever. Now I listen to the music, and I find I appreciate it more."

At the table next to us, a woman started singing quietly to the small child sat next to her in a push-chair. The song was 'Banbury Cross'. Paul asked me what I was laughing about, and I told him about my black hole when it came to nursery rhymes.

"That's nothing," he replied. "When I was little, there was a song called *Who's Sorry Now*. I think it was by Connie Francis. And for years I thought Sorry Now was a real person. You know – Who is Sorry Now? I couldn't work out who this person was, and why this woman was singing about her.

"Then there was another one, *Faith Can Move Mountains* by Johnny Ray. Well, good for her. But I had an older cousin called Faith who lived somewhere down near Northampton, where there were no mountains. Try working that out when you're five years old."

I left Sutton sometime after lunch, the temperature nudging 80 degrees according to one of those digital display boards you find tacked to the side of high-rise office blocks. I motored towards Tamworth with every available window open. Morris Minors don't know the meaning of the words 'air' and 'conditioned', and besides that the dirty-linen bag in the back seat was beginning to hum. I'd been putting off visiting a launderette, relying instead on the seemingly bottomless pit of tennis clothes stashed away in the car boot. But now, one clean shirt away from playing topless, finding one was becoming a priority.

Now if you're reading this and come from Tamworth, or have any affinity with the town, I must apologise for somehow managing to drive through it without noticing. The road signs tempt you in – 'Tamworth 5 miles', 'Tamworth 3 miles', plenty of roundabouts, retail parks – and then suddenly you're out the other side. Congratulations to whoever built the ring road – it does its job so well you don't even realise you're on it. Which means Tamworth is probably one step away from becoming somewhere like Leatherdead. And if that's the case, I'm glad I missed it.

I did find two courts on the northern edge of town belonging to Queen Elizabeth Lower School. But like my old secondary school, the nets had been taken down to create extra car-parking space. A group of parents stood beside them, waiting for their little ones to come charging out at 3pm. One, a youngish woman with blonde hair called Maggie, agreed to have a hit with me around a Citroen 2CV and two Volvo Estates, to the amusement of all the other mums.

"Do you have kids of your own?" she asked.

I told her one was on its way.

"You'll love it. It can be hard work, but it's something you'll never regret. Do you know if it's going to be a he or a she?"

"No, I don't, but I've got a feeling it's going to be a girl. I can't say why. Just a hunch."

"So where's your wife while you're out doing this?"

"She's back in Yorkshire, working as a teacher."

"And she doesn't mind you being away?"

"Not that I know of, no."

"Well I hope you'll be around to do your bit after it's born. Life changes then, you know? You won't find enough time to sleep, let alone play tennis."

And at that moment Maggie's little boy ran up, grabbed her by the hand and whisked her off.

I took the black and white scan picture out of my wallet, the one we'd had taken in Pontefract Hospital two days before I started my trip. No matter how hard I looked, it was impossible to make anything out besides a bit of leg. The rest was just a fuzzy mass where the foetus was meant to be, like one of those underwater pictures supposedly showing the Loch Ness Monster. In the three weeks since the picture was taken, he or she had probably grown by another five and a quarter ounces, developed enough muscle to do the odd loop-the-loop inside Alex's womb, yet still had plenty of room to move within the amniotic sac (don't ask me). How did I know all this? Because while hanging around on tennis courts waiting for victims to come along, I'd been reading my *Rough Guide To Pregnancy and Birth*. And very interesting it was too. I also knew my wife would soon be suffering from backache, and that her waistline had undoubtedly started to go AWOL (though judging from our daily, evening phone-calls, she was definitely in denial about this).

I discovered two more tennis courts that afternoon – one in a picturesque village called Newton Regis, the other in Measham. On both occasions they were locked up, with no way of finding out who had a key. So in true All England Club style, I wrote 'The Server Woz Here' on a pair of old tennis balls, and knocked them over the fence onto the tarmac. Coming out of Measham, I passed a sign for Ashby de la Zouch, which up until then I'd always believed was a fictional land, a bit like Gotham City or Narnia. Always a sucker for completely barking place-names, I decided to drive there and find somewhere to stay the night.

"Ah, you're French!" said Jocelyne, the French co-owner of the Ashby Court Hotel in Wood Street, copying down the name on my credit card.

"No. I'm part Welsh, part English, part Norwegian. But I'm not French. Vignes is actually a Norwegian surname."

"No, it's not," she replied. "Vignes is the French word for 'grape', or 'grapevine' to be more exact. Somebody in your family must have been French. Perhaps they moved to Norway many, many years ago. But you are French."

"I don't think so."

"*Yes, you are!*"

My family history is confusing to say the least, but nobody had ever mentioned anything to me about a French connection before. My grandfather was originally a merchant seaman from the Norwegian port of Stavanger. When the Germans invaded the country during World War Two, most of the ships had managed to escape to British ports, including Cardiff. John Vignes was one of those who ended up in the Welsh capital. He married a local girl, had a son (my father), who in turn eventually married a Londoner. And then I came along.

As a kid, I was always immensely proud of my mixed-up heritage. It meant I could play sport at international level for one of three different countries. My father had always considered the English to be an arrogant bunch, and from an early age he did a pretty good job of brainwashing me into all things Welsh. Which I was more than happy with, despite my birthday falling on St George's Day. Growing up in Sussex and saying you were Welsh was a way of showing you were *different*. Wales had Gareth Edwards and Richard Burton.

England had Emlyn Hughes (despite his name) and Roger Moore. It was no contest.

Now, in my 34th year, a complete stranger was telling me that I was also French. Don't get me wrong. I like France as a place to visit, and I've met some very nice people over there. But in no way do I want to be French. Was this something my father and grandfather had deliberately kept from me, a secret they'd both taken to the grave? My father always liked practical jokes. Nine years after his death, perhaps he'd just played the biggest one of all.

I found a launderette in Market Street and left my clothes spinning round while I went for a walk to get over the French business. Ashby Castle sounded like a good place to kill an hour, so I followed the signposts which led me to – Ashby Lawn Tennis Club. Apparently the castle had sold off some land to create a tennis club at the beginning of the last century. So seven courts now stood where hangings and jousting once took place. Dressed in jeans and a sweatshirt, and without my racket, I decided to return later for a knock after I'd had a look around what remained of the castle.

Which proved to be very little but the odd wall here and there. Whoever destroyed it had done a pretty thorough job. There seemed to be more information boards dotted around than bricks. One of them (a board, not a brick) carried a fascinating tale about Sir Walter Scott, who in 1819 had stopped in Ashby to see a friend called Sir George Beaumont. Beaumont lived in a big house just outside the village called Coleorton Hall. While strolling around the grounds one day, Scott had been inspired to write the novel *Ivanhoe*, his first based anywhere outside Scotland. Apparently the jousting tournament where Ivanhoe and Richard I squared up against Prince John's groupies was based at Ashby, in all probability on the land now occupied by the tennis club. And soon, according to an old guy walking a labrador around the ruins, Coleorton Hall was to be converted into some expensive luxury flats, having served as the local headquarters for the National Union of Mineworkers for the best part of a century.

Right, that's enough history. Washing done and collected, I returned to the tennis club after dinner at the hotel to see if anyone fancied a match. However, Ashby were taking on the mighty Kibworth in a Leicestershire league match that evening, and every court was occupied. This was serious stuff, and I was an unwelcome distraction. Nobody cared about my trip or a possible starring role in a book, and I got the distinct impression they wished I'd just go away.

"Why don't you come back tomorrow," said one guy who carried with him the air of being someone rather important in the men's first team. "There'll be plenty of people down here in the evening. You can play for fun then."

Oh dear. Two problems with that, Mr Condescending I'm Wearing All The Latest Expensive Gear And Playing With A Racket Worth More Than Most People's Car. First, the assumption that I was nothing but a 'fun' player. I'd take that from Lleyton Hewitt, not you, mate. Second, what made him think I'd want to hang around his scabby little tennis club for 24 hours on the off-chance of getting a hit?

A couple of women from the Ladies Doubles 'B' team must have seen the red mist descending across my face, and stepped in to ask if I wouldn't mind rallying with them until their opponents arrived. I agreed, and got five minutes worth of action before Kibworth 'B' showed up. Not one person so much as looked in my direction, or even offered a 'Goodbye', as I left.

Back in the hotel bar, completely at a loose end following the tennis club snub, I got chatting to Lars and Lennart from Sweden. Both were big tennis and classic-car fans, and were making an overnight stop on their way home from visiting the Morgan sports car factory in the Worcestershire town of Malvern. Outside in the car park, their Volvo Estate was full to bursting point with spare parts destined for other members of the Swedish branch of the Morgan Owners Club.

The beer flowed, followed by a couple of bottles of wine and a rather heated discussion about who was the better player – Bjorn Borg or his Swedish compatriot Stefan Edberg.

Lars: "I always thought Borg was a good player, but he had nothing on Stefan Edberg. Edberg was the greatest, and he played at a time when the players around him were better and the game was faster."

Me: "How can you say that? Borg won Wimbledon five times in a row, not to mention the French Open six times in eight years."

Lars: "Yes, but he never won the US or the Australian Opens. Stefan won both of them – twice. Another bottle of red?

Me: "Oh yeah, definitely. What do you reckon, Lennart?

Lennart: "I think that Mats Wilander was better than both of them."

Me/Lars (together): "MATS WILANDER!"

There's a rather odd postscript to this story. The following evening, the ferry that Lars and Lennart had been on their way to catch from Newcastle caught fire in the North Sea. A major rescue operation was launched involving the RAF, the Royal Navy, the Norwegian rescue services and workers from a number of oil rigs. Thankfully no-one died, and the boat managed to limp into a port in Norway. Which just goes to show – never get into an argument with me over tennis. Because if I don't like what I hear, I will put a curse on you. And your ferry.

Mellowed by wine and some fine company, I decided to give Ashby Tennis Club a second chance the next morning. Perhaps I'd been a little harsh on them the night before. I wouldn't like it if some chatty freak in search of a rally came sniffing round me minutes before an important match, destroying my concentration. My cold had completely cleared up and the elbow seemed to be behaving itself, so I was in the mood for a few sets.

I'm glad I did. Three men had turned up for a game of doubles, a fourth having been held up at a business meeting in Leicester. For once, I was in the right place at the right time, and made up the numbers. We played a couple of sets, pausing for a short respite at the end of the first to change partners. During the break, I started talking to the one player who was head and shoulders better than the rest of us. This bloke was a former Wimbledon umpire and line judge, full of stories and opinions on the game, most of which were fabulously libellous. I got the feeling he'd told them all a thousand times before, yet they were still interesting. And, as he remained a member of the LTA and didn't want to ruffle any feathers, he begged me to use a pseudonym. So Mr White it is.

"I gave it all up because it became more hassle than it was worth," he said. "I was there from the mid-seventies up until 1987, which you could call the 'golden age' of tennis. So I got to sit in on all the big names, including the Borg and McEnroe finals of 1980 and 1981. But the abuse we had to put up with was ridiculous. All for our £30 match fee and two complimentary tickets for family and friends.

"McEnroe and Fleming (Peter) were bad, but they weren't the worst. That honour went to a doubles pair called McMillan and Hewitt. They were terrible. Constant backchat, questioning every decision. But it wasn't just them. There were plenty of players who went out of their way to give you a hard time. It wasn't uncommon to see officials close to tears."

Really? Any examples?

"I remember one match, involving Jimmy Connors, when a lady was in the umpire's chair. I'll spare her the embarrassment of naming her. There had been a couple of close line-calls, which Connors hadn't liked, and he'd questioned them. He could see she was getting in a state. After one particularly close call, Connors put his racket between his legs and moved his fingers up and down the grip. You know, making a 'wanker' sign. And she gave him a warning. So Connors comes back over to the chair to ask why. He knew he had her, because she'd be too embarrassed to say. They eventually carried on playing, but she had lost all control over the match. At the next change round, she was replaced by another umpire. Can you imagine having to put up with that, the shame of it? All for just a few pounds."

Rather than tell him I was still Jimmy Connors's biggest fan, I sought his opinion on the Swedish debate from the previous evening.

"Borg or Edberg? Oh Borg, without a doubt. He was so consistent, and brilliant with it. You know, he had his own practice court at home where the lines had been narrowed by three inches? That way, whenever he went out and played on a normal court, he was always sure of keeping the ball in. He was a genius. But he wasn't the best. McEnroe is still the most technically brilliant player I've ever seen. That Wimbledon final of 1984 when he beat Connors, making only three unforced errors throughout. That's as good as it gets."

As the second set drew to a close, the missing fourth player turned up. Which I was gutted about, as I had just started to hit a few decent shots after a diabolical start. I collected my gear and thanked them all for their time.

"What's your name again?" asked Mr White.

I told him.

"What's that, French?"

CHAPTER TEN

Derby Days

**"There is something of an intense rivalry
between Derby and Nottingham, and Derby
often comes out second best on most counts."**
Lonely Planet Guide to Britain

On the afternoon of December 7th 2000, 82-year-
old Mr James Mulligan of Cheshunt, Hertfordshire,
set off on what should have been a 25-minute drive
home from his daughter's house in the nearby town
of Bishop's Stortford. Intending to pull off the
southbound carriageway of the M11 motorway
before its junction with the M25, Mr Mulligan
missed his turn and became lost on London's
notoriously scary orbital road. When he still hadn't
returned home later that evening, his wife
Catherine alerted the police, who warned patrol
cars to be on the lookout out for his H-registration
Ford Fiesta.

At some point Mr Mulligan did manage to find an exit, only to run out of petrol. He was found, dazed and confused, standing beside a road in the London borough of Hackney, some 27 hours after leaving his daughter's house. It later emerged that this was the second time the M25 had led Mr Mulligan astray. The previous year, he had circled London for a whole day and night before being rescued by police.

As the Morris nosed its way through the maze of roads where the M1 meets the A42 near East Midlands Airport, I caught a glimpse of how our hero might have got himself in such a pickle. To my right, the M1 to London and the A42/M42 for Birmingham. On my left, the M1 north. Behind me, the road I'd just driven along and a runway, a Boeing 737 bearing down on Moggie's back bumper as it taxied for take-off. Desperate to stick to the back lanes, I skim-read the multi-lingual signs telling me to 'Links fahren' and 'Tenez la gauche' for an escape route. Salvation came with a small arrow pointing the way over the M1 to Kegworth. *Kegworth* – now there was a name I'd forgotten about. One synonymous with death and that horrible rash of disasters which occurred during the mid-eighties and the early to mid nineties – Hungerford, Dunblane, Bradford, Kings Cross, Lockerbie, Clapham, Zeebrugge, Hillsborough. For some strange reason, those names still remained imprinted on the brain – Kegworth hadn't.

It was in January 1989 that flight BD092 from Heathrow to Belfast developed engine problems 10 minutes after leaving London. Diverted to East Midlands Airport, the aircraft had limped over the rooftops of Kegworth before crashing into an embankment on the M1. Forty-seven people died, yet incredibly 79 survived. Driving down the High Street in the Morris 13 years later, holiday jets cruising in to land above me, it was easy to see how the disaster could have been so much worse. Another quarter of a mile to the east, and BD092 would have taken out much of the village.

I've always felt slightly uneasy visiting places forever blighted by some kind of disaster. Ten years after the Hungerford massacre of 1987, when a local firearms fanatic went on the rampage killing 14 people, I wrote an article on how the residents of the Berkshire town had come to terms with what happened. Interviews had been prearranged with witnesses and survivors, so it wasn't as though I was cornering people out of the blue, or 'door-stepping' as it's called in the media. Yet it was still one of the toughest assignments I've ever done, simply because I felt like a ghoul, no better than the sick day-trippers who came to retrace the gunman's steps, looking for bullet marks on cottage walls. Or the tourists on their way to Bath, pointing sympathetically from their cosy air-conditioned coaches at a community now inexorably linked with death, all because of some trigger-happy misfit.

So there I was being a ghoul all over again, this time in Kegworth. I hadn't planned on going there. It was just the way my journey had panned out. I parked the Morris outside Ye Olde Flying Horse pub and went into a paper shop to buy a can of drink and some chocolate. The man behind the counter looked friendly. I wanted to greet him with a cheerful "Weather's a bit dull for May" line, but knew the moment I opened my mouth it would come out as "I'm so sorry about what happened. How are you all now?" In the confusion, I ended up saying nothing. Like everybody else, he probably just wanted to get on with his life, not have the past dragged up by moronic, well-intentioned but unwelcome visitors like me.

Back in the Morris, cruising about looking for somewhere pleasant to stop and munch my snacks, I came across Kegworth Tennis Club. Surrounded by a full-scale Colditz-replica fence, even a serve looked out of the question unless someone turned up with a key or a pair of industrial-strength wire-cutters. I set the stopwatch running and started eating, a map of the East Midlands area open on my lap. From Kegworth, I could either head north-west towards Derby and the Peak District beyond it, or north-east to Nottingham and up through Sherwood Forest. I had to make some kind of decision other-wise I'd end up on the M1 doing a Mr Mulligan.

Tea break over, and with eight of my 20 minutes remaining, I began playing wall ball against the village hall to pass the time, directly beneath a large sign saying 'No Ball Games'. After a while, I realised I was being watched by a small person licking an ice cream. I said hello and asked its name.

"Jake."

"Hello, Jake. Do you like tennis?"

"Don't know."

"Would you like a go?"

He nodded. I handed over my racket and Jake began gently knocking the ball against the wall, scraping my beautifully kept Donnay along the gravel floor with every other stroke.

"Do you like living in Kegworth, Jake?"

"Yes."

"What do you like about it?"

"Um... don't know."

"Do you have many friends here?"

"Yes."

"Derby or Nottingham?"

"Derby."

Poor sod. He thought I was asking what his favourite football team was – Derby County or Nottingham Forest. Never mind. So Jake solved my direction dilemma, and taught me a valuable lesson in the process – if you ever visit somewhere haunted by the past, and are worried about how to talk to the locals without sounding like a disaster package tourist, corner somebody who wasn't even born when the disaster happened.

Just as I was preparing to scribble a note onto the ball and lob it over the tennis club fence, a car drew up and out got Ian. I knew his name was Ian because the IKEA badge on his disgustingly bright yellow work shirt said so. Out came the spiel, and he told me Kegworth had an away fixture that evening against a team from Leicester. The team was meeting at the clubhouse before travelling there in convoy for a 6.30pm start.

Ian gave me permission to serve a ball on the club's courts, but declined my offer of a quick rally (obviously scared that I'd exhaust him before his big match). We stood about chatting, waiting for the rest of the team to arrive, and I told him the story of my trip so far. He seemed really interested, so interested that I was waiting for the bit where he said, "I tell you what – come and play for Kegworth tonight. We could do with a swashbuckling, big-serving guy like yourself." And I would have done. The elbow was staying the pace, and after a day of wall ball and trying to avoid 737s, I felt in the mood for a proper match, one with league positions and points at stake.

The offer never came. Three other players all arrived within a few minutes of each other, and together with Ian they all disappeared off inside the clubhouse to get changed and talk about 'rubbers'. Stop sniggering at the back there. The word is basically tennis-speak for inter-club matches, and has nothing to do with any kind of contraceptive.

I was on my own again, all dressed up with no-one to play. I pulled out my mobile phone and called a friend who lived a few miles away in Long Eaton, hoping for a bed for the night. She was in and up to her eyeballs in decorating. I could stay on two conditions. One, that I brought a bottle of wine and some takeaway with me. Two, that I helped with some wallpaper stripping. Seemed like a fair deal to me.

Jake had obviously been taught at school that the wettest place in the British Isles isn't Fort William, that place in the Lake District that no-one ever remembers the name of, or even Banbury – it's Derby. So apart from taking a few chunks out of my racket, the little toe-rag also sent me off directly into the path of the 'perfect storm' – driving rain, extras standing off-screen hurling buckets of water over you, the whole shebang.

It began spitting on the morning of Day 20 while I was at Grove Farm, a beautiful house in the Derby suburb of Thulston with a tennis court in the garden. The owners were away on holiday, but Graham the carpenter was about and let me take a serve. At least he said he was the carpenter. My apologies to the owners for not making a citizen's arrest if they returned to a burgled house. While I was standing there on the baseline, sizing up where to place the shot, I felt the first drop of rain land on my forearm. By the time I'd said goodbye to Graham and returned to the car, it was teeming down. I drove into the city where I took refuge in the Eagle Centre, full of your standard run-of-the-mill chain stores selling mobile phone accessories, mass-produced jewellery and CDs by manufactured bands with a combined age of 12.

This conversation really took place in one of those stores. I'll call it a record shop, even though you can't buy the things any more, as CD shop doesn't really have the same ring. For lovers of Roxy Music and their lead singer, I suggest you look away now.

Me: "Hi. Can you tell me, do you have the new album by Bryan Ferry in stock, because I can't see it anywhere on the shelves?"

Young Female Shop Assistant: "I'll go and check for you."

Brief interlude while YFSA goes in search of album.

YFSA (looking baffled): "What name did you say again?"

Me: "Bryan Ferry"

YFSA: "Is he a new artist?"

Holy poker! Here was someone who didn't know who Bryan Ferry was. I felt a mixture of anger and amazement, followed closely by the icy claw of a premature mid-life crisis. Was it *that* long since Bryan last released an album? I wouldn't have been able to listen to it anyway, even if she had been able to find it. Morris Minors don't come with CD players, and albums on cassette were phased out around the same time as Bjorn Borg launched his 24th comeback. It's just that traditionally, I've always bought the new album by any of my favourite bands or singers on the day of its release: partly out of loyalty to the artist, partly as a legacy from my school days when it was a trendy thing to do. Oh well, it's a tradition that Derby and its musically-challenged record-shop staff put a stop to.

I spent the afternoon trapped inside the Eagle. The rain meant tennis and looking for a B&B were no-nos, unless I fancied getting drenched by the tidal waves battering the skylights above me. I bought a stack of papers and spent a couple of hours in the food court drinking coffee at £1.60 a shot. When I'd read every word in the sports and obituary sections, I turned to people-watching. Which didn't last very long, as everyone was dressed head to toe in waterproofs, their faces blinkered by cone-shaped hoods. Bored and caffeined up to the eyeballs, I made a run for it back to the car and drove around looking for a place to stay.

It wasn't long before I spotted a 'Rooms Available' sign on a window near the station: 'Bed only, no breakfast, 25 quid a night'. The manageress showed me my single room, which was small but bearable, then asked me to sign the register.

And for some reason, I wrote the name Kevin Curren, one of my favourite tennis players of the eighties and the man who lost to Becker in the Wimbledon final of 1985. Now I'd love to say that the real reason I did this was because I didn't want anyone else mistaking me for a Frenchman. But it wasn't. I just wanted to have a bit of a laugh and check in somewhere under a pseudonym. Childish, I grant you, but a bit of fun.

That evening the rain finally eased and Kevin Curren decided to go on a drive around Derby looking for courts. After a couple of miles, I discovered ten of them together, slap-bang in the middle of a factory complex, to the south of the city centre. They belonged to the Rolls Royce Welfare Club, and were there to be used by company employees and their families.

I introduced myself to the nearest person, who happened to be a girl in her late teens called Polly Allsop. Her father, Geoff, had recently retired after 42 years working for Rolls Royce. Polly should have been inside revising for her impending 'A' level exams, but had decided to go out and play a few sets instead. That's what I like to see – a girl getting her priorities right.

Despite the dank weather, plenty of other people were arriving and changing from their work clothes into tennis gear. Some were taking part in a league game against a club from Sheffield, and once again I started getting my hopes up that maybe I'd be invited onto the team. It wasn't to be, but I couldn't really complain. They were such a nice bunch, and I ended up playing two sets of doubles with other club members before the rain started again and everyone made a dash for their cars and home. Everyone that is except the dozen or so drowned rats involved in the league game, who kept on playing despite the occasional clap of thunder. I sat watching them from the veranda outside the club pavilion, chatting to a guy called Andrew, who had travelled down with the Sheffield club as a reserve player.

"There used to be this unofficial league up in Sheffield, which my father played in, that was basically a drinking league," he said. "During each match you would pick up fines, which were punishable by having a drink. Like if I served a double fault, I'd have to down a pint, and so on. You even had to drink a pint after finishing each set. I think the local tennis association banned it in the end."

"That's one way of getting people in this country to take up tennis as a sport," I replied.

"Yeah, but the standard of play was never very good, ha ha! Imagine that. Grand Slam tournaments like Wimbledon and Flushing Meadows for pissheads only. We might have a chance of winning something then!"

As I was leaving, I bumped into Geoff Allsop, who had come to collect his daughter. A teetotaller, he declined my offer of a drink in the clubhouse, so instead we sat and talked out of the rain in his Ford Escort.

"Years ago all of the factories around here had social facilities like these – tennis, cricket, amateur dramatics, bowls, choir, you name it," he said. "But as businesses got smaller and budgets got tighter, those were the kind of things that management got rid of. Of course, some factories shut down altogether. So now Rolls Royce is one of a kind. It looks after its employees, which is the way it should be, right?"

"Right."

"You know, everywhere you go in the world, people have heard of Derby, and it's usually because of the railways, Brian Clough or Rolls Royce. We design and assemble aircraft engines here, so times are a little tough at the moment. Two thousand people were laid off after September 11th, all because of orders being put on hold. But we'll bounce back."

Whenever I hear the name Brian Clough, I tend to think more of Nottingham, not Derby. And when it comes to railways, you can't beat Crewe. But he seemed so proud of his home city that I wasn't going to argue.

The next morning I was up bright and early to find somewhere to have breakfast. So early that nowhere besides the railway-station buffet seemed open. I ordered a sausage, bacon and egg sandwich and sat down to read a copy of the previous day's *Derby Evening Telegraph*. Later that morning, six Rolls Royce Silver Spirits would be driving around the city in a publicity stunt organised by the National Lottery. Apparently, somebody had bought a winning ticket in Derby two months earlier, and had yet to claim their £3.4 million prize. Each Spirit had been assigned one of the lucky numbers, which would be displayed on posters plastered to every available inch of paintwork. The paper also claimed that since the National Lottery started in 1994, nearly £464 million in winnings had gone unclaimed – almost as much as the All England Club seem to make every minute during Wimbledon.

As I ate my sandwich, I took out a pen and some paper and wrote down a few meaningless statistics about the trip so far. In 20 days, I'd:

- covered 255 miles
- hit a ball on 95 different courts (one for every 2.68 miles, if my maths was correct)
- found someone to rally against on 51 occasions (52 if you include the enthusiastic tabby cat in Perivale)
- 47 of those 51 had been either white or of Anglo-Saxon origin
- four had been Asian (all Korean)

None had been black. Not one.

I even tried to add up how many games I'd played (not to be confused with sets), but gave up at 226. No wonder my elbow had been giving me grief.

I returned to my lodgings to pack my bag, settle my bill and revel in a "Goodbye, Mr Curren" from the duty manager. Driving down King Street, I caught sight of lottery numbers 17, 18 and 35 in the Rolls Royce convoy passing in the opposite direction. No sign whatsoever of 32, 39 and 48. They'd probably overheated in the stop-start mid-morning traffic. Wouldn't have happened if they'd used Moggie Minors.

The landscape began to change dramatically after Derby. The flat, open expanse of the East Midlands steadily made way for the rolling, green hills at the southern end of the Peak District. Beautiful scenery, but a pain in the arse if you're searching for tennis courts which, as you don't have to be a brain surgeon to appreciate, need to be built on flat land.

Near the village of Duffield, I decided to check out a signpost pointing the way to a sports ground, and found myself stranded in a dead-end lane outside St Alkmund's Church. As I attempted to three-point turn my way out of trouble, a large Rolls Royce (do they drive anything else up here?) pulled up and a bride stepped out, accompanied by a man who I presumed was her father. Behind them, another Rolls arrived carrying three bridesmaids. As I sat there, boxed in and wondering what the hell to do, everyone including the drivers raced off into the church. Whether I liked it or not, I was at a wedding.

I got out of the car to see if there was enough room for me to manoeuvre the Morris past the two Rolls with the help of a grass verge. There wasn't.

A late arrival hurried past, as fast as you can possibly go in three-foot heels.

"You're not going dressed like that, are you?"

"I'm not going at all," I replied. And before I could ask her to send the owners of RR 250 and RR 255 outside to move their cars, she'd gone.

Dying of embarrassment and wanting to get on my way, I paced around the graveyard trying to decide what to do. From inside the church came the sound of a soloist's voice. I edged my way to the entrance and peered in. A young girl, probably about ten years old, was standing at the front facing the happy couple. She was singing *Somewhere Over The Rainbow*. Not one of my favourite songs, but her voice was absolutely beautiful. And she held that difficult last note perfectly, the one that accompanies the '*Why Then Oh Why Can't I...?*'. The women were crying, the men busy pretending not to. And at the end everyone applauded loudly, including me.

Just then one of the limousine drivers appeared behind me smoking a cigarette. I told him my predicament, and asked if he could move the cars. He went to find his fellow driver, and the Rolls were moved just far enough for me to squeeze out. I never did find the sports ground.

On the Moggie rolled, through Belper, Ambergate and Cromford. Lovely places, all built halfway up hills, no tennis courts. None that I could find anyway. From the car radio, just to dampen my spirits even further, came a gale warning for all routes over the Peak District and the Pennines. Whoever invented that old saying 'It's like pissing in the wind' probably did so to describe their frustration at trying to serve a tennis ball in a force six. The thing is usually halfway to China before your racket has gone above head height. You'd be lucky to get a set completed inside three years.

By mid-afternoon I'd reached Matlock, popular with the Victorians as it reminded them of Switzerland. Not too sure why. Not a mountain goat, ski-run or cuckoo clock in sight. But it looked a nice enough place to spend the night. The first B&B I came across was fully booked, but the manager was generous enough to give me a spare leaflet called *Accommodation in Matlock 2002*. I sat and studied it in the car. Each one seemed to be trying to outdo the other with starring roles in various films or TV series. For instance, 'Hill View, a traditional Victorian house, as featured in the film *Women in Love*, conveniently located for the town centre'. Or 'Riverbank House, a tranquil spot only minutes from all amenities, as featured in *Peak Practice*'.

In the end, *Peak Practice* came out on top, as I'd spotted two courts close by in Hall Leys Park. I unloaded the car and found my room on the second floor, passing various pictures dotted up the stairway of the *Peak Practice* production team doing their stuff around the house. I was just looking forward to five minutes in the little boys' room with *The Guardian* when there was a knock at the door.

"Terribly sorry, but I forgot to ask you to sign the register. Could you come down and do it when you've got a moment?"

I sure could. Any excuse to adopt a pseudonym and become a man of mystery for the second time in as many nights. The name 'John Newcombe' was just about to go on the dotted line when I had a sudden brainwave. Perhaps one day, having established myself as a rich and famous writer, Riverbank House would want to become 'a tranquil spot only minutes from all amenities, as featured in the Spencer Vignes bestseller *The Server*'? So I wrote my own name.

Although my right shoulder was feeling tight from the previous night's action at the Rolls Royce Welfare Club, I still hoped I might bump into somebody at the park who would be up for a serious match. So I'm sorry, Mr Trevor Gill, a retired pensioner from Matlock who hadn't played tennis in over 40 years, if I appeared a little reticent during our shambolic five-minute contest. Next time, it might help if you remembered your glasses for the daily walk to the shops.

"Why don't you try the local tennis club on the Bakewell Road?" he said, as we shook hands at the net. "You might get a better game up there."

So I went in search of this club, eventually finding myself a couple of miles outside town in the grounds of St Elphin's School. And by the time I got there, the wind was seriously beginning to pick up. The two courts, dug into the side of a hill, were exposed to say the least. Yet two young men were trying their best to play a match. Their names were Richard and Seb. Richard was in the forces, in the process of transferring from the Navy to the Royal Marines, and enjoying a few days home leave.

"We're not actually members of the club," he said. "It's just that these courts are only used a couple of evenings a week, so when I'm back the two of us often come down for a game. I bet you haven't played anywhere with a view like this on your trip."

I hadn't. The scenery both up the valley towards Bakewell and back towards Matlock was certainly spectacular. Seb kindly offered to step aside while Richard and I played a set, which was a pretty stupid thing to do given the conditions. It wasn't a serious match, and the two of us chatted throughout about my journey and his career in the Navy. Only I wasn't able to pick up much of what he said. The wind was just too strong. From the opposite side of the net, I could see his mouth moving, but couldn't hear the words. Judging by what I could make of his responses, he was having much the same problem.

"So how long were you in the Navy?"

"About 10 minutes."

"You must have visited a lot of interesting places then."

"Yeah, as tennis courts go they're not too bad."

"Are you looking forward to joining the Royal Marines then?"

"About twenty-five to eight."

Having taken almost an hour to complete just five measly games, we decided to call it a day. I wished him all the best on his career in the Marines, and drove back to Matlock.

That evening I decided to stay off the takeaway burgers and treat myself to dinner at The Strand restaurant – striking black and white colour scheme, good selection of bottled beer and proper old-fashioned jazz on the in-house stereo, not the Kenny G musical-wank variety. The place was reasonably full for a Wednesday night, and while wolfing down my steak I began scanning the room to see if I was in the presence of any 'look-a-likes'. Well, it helps pass the time when you're travelling on your own. And my luck was in – a dead ringer for K. D. Lang was sitting to my left, talking TV programmes with a female friend.

Now I've always hated the way travel writers often mock people they encounter for the pettiest of things, like the way they hold a cup of tea or pronounce 'Newcastle'. It's nearly always done from the safety of an office at home, behind their victims' backs, rather than face to face. I suppose I should also plead guilty to this – witness my rant at the Derby shop assistant. That in mind, I was to feel pretty ashamed about what happened next.

Tucking into my apple-pie, I realised that the middle-aged couple at the next table hadn't said a word to each other since I arrived. Over half-an-hour of quiet, broken only by the sound of cutlery on china plates and the occasional cough. The longer this silence went on, the louder and more intriguing it became. Perhaps they'd had the mother of all arguments before going out, one that any second now would recommence in a massive food fight. Maybe it was some kind of bet that had got out of control – you know, next one to speak pays the bill and does the washing up for a month. Lost in my smug little world, I recalled a scene from the Monty Python film *The Meaning of Life* where a waiter, played by John Cleese, invites couples to pick a subject to talk about over dinner, 20 years of marriage having left them stuck for conversation. Perhaps I could offer these two 'Who had the worst hair – Borg or Gerulaitis?', or 'Anna Kournikova – all image, no substance. Discuss.'

Then, within seconds of me scribbling 'Weird Mute Couple' on a paper napkin as a reminder for this chapter, something truly unsettling happened. The woman began to cry. Not just a few tears accompanied by the odd sniff, but a fully-fledged, no holds-barred sob. The man, slightly embarrassed, reached across the table to take hold of her hands. She discreetly pushed him away. He tried again, only to be rebuffed once more. Soon everyone in the place knew of her discomfort. Table by table, all conversation died, until the only audible voice belonged to Peggy Lee singing *They Can't Take That Away From Me* on the restaurant stereo.

The couple continued to sit there for another few minutes, rivers running down the woman's face and onto the tablecloth, the sound of her sobbing entwined with Peggy's silky vocals. Still no words were exchanged. It was horrible to watch. Eventually she got up, put her coat on and walked out. He sat there, looking blankly at the empty space opposite him. Eventually, a sympathetic waitress came over to ask if everything was all right. He nodded, paid the bill, and left. And I sat there, shell-shocked, feeling like a right bastard.

****

That night I had the strangest dream, one that thankfully brightened my mood after the restaurant incident (though what it said about my tennis-drenched state-of-mind, I'll leave up to you).

I was walking through a cemetery with Goran Ivanisevic, the man who got so excited after winning Wimbledon in 2001 that he stripped down to his underpants in front of 150,000 jubilant Croatians on returning to his home town of Split. As you do.

Eventually the two of us came to a bar in what I presumed was Matlock, as it looked a bit like The Strand from the previous evening. We went inside and ordered a couple of beers. In the corner, Chris de Burgh was singing his hit *Missing You*. He finished, paused briefly and went into his next number. It was *Missing You* again.

This continued until Chris, caught in some kind of loop, had performed the song another five times. By now Goran, clearly not the world's biggest De Burgh fan, was seething. He started muttering dark threats in Croatian – well, I presume they must have been Croatian, as I couldn't understand a word he was saying.

As Chris launched into rendition number six, Goran decided he could stand it no longer. Handing me his beer, he waded through the crowd to the small stage where the singer was standing. And he chinned him. A big, full-blooded punch that sent the little Irish crooner spinning through the air into some tables and chairs. I'd love to tell you what happened next but at that point I woke up laughing.

Still, it could've been worse for Chris. At least it wasn't *Lady In Red*. The opening bars of that and the whole place would've been queuing up behind Goran to take a swipe.

CHAPTER ELEVEN

Tarts

"Don't look at age, look at ability."
Martina Navratilova, still playing at 46

Nancy Hathaway was 81 years old before she picked up a tennis racket for the first time. A keen armchair fan of the game, she never failed to watch Wimbledon on TV every summer from her home in the Derbyshire town of Bakewell. But that was as far as her relationship with the sport went.

Then one morning in May 2002, a weird thing happened. While out walking through the local park with her two labradors, Penny and Jessie, she was approached by a strange man. He garbled something about Burt Lancaster and a journey, and handed her a tennis racket. Nancy took a good look at him. He seemed sane enough, nothing like the shifty actors on those *Crimewatch* reconstructions. Anyway, if he did try anything funny, she now had a tennis racket to beat him over the head with.

Before Nancy knew it, she was on a court hitting a ball backwards and forwards with the strange man. And having fun.

"It's quite easy, isn't it?" she said.

The strange man had to agree – she was a natural. One by one, Nancy's elderly friends came out of their bungalows surrounding the park to cheer her on.

"I'd better go and call Wimbledon about you, see if they'll let you play this year," one of them called out. "We could all go down to London for the day to watch!"

"You know, it's funny. I've walked past these courts a thousand times, and never once thought about stopping to have a game. Then you turn up and I discover I quite like it. I suppose it's a bit late now, at my age."

Jessie, sprawled on the grass by the tennis court gates, slowly raised her head and gave me a withering look. One that had 'ever since you arrived, I've been neglected' written all over it. I asked Nancy to tell me about Bakewell, and in particular the town's famous tarts.

"They're not tarts. They're puddings. You have to get it right."

All-righty-then.

"There are plenty of shops in the town that make puddings, but the one you really need to look out for is The Old Original Bakewell Pudding Shop. That's where it all started. Go to the roundabout and turn right towards the tourist information building. You can't miss it."

I wanted to thank Nancy for being such a tremendous sport by giving her a present – a copy of Vince's *Music To Smash Heads By* perhaps. If nothing else, it might encourage her to carry on playing for years to come. But she wasn't having any of it.

"If you hadn't come to Bakewell, I would probably have gone through life without playing tennis. I'm the one who should be thanking you!"

I followed Nancy's directions and found the pudding shop straightaway. A line of people stretched out of the door, waiting patiently to get their paws on the bizarre-looking pastries, a cross between a custard tart (oh God, I've said the forbidden word) and a flan. Stuck to a wall just inside the entrance was a newspaper feature on the history of the pudding. Now don't take this as gospel, but allegedly a cook at The Rutland Arms, the town's most famous hotel, screwed up his egg mixture while trying to make a strawberry tart, and HEY PRESTO! The Bakewell Pudding was born. The feature also said that the exact recipe was a closely-guarded secret.

I joined the queue snaking around the extensive range of pudding-related souvenirs on offer. Many, including plates and mugs, bore the words 'THE SECRET RECIPE', together with the exact ingredients needed to make a pudding.

"That doesn't really make it a secret, does it?" I said to the girl taking orders behind the counter.

"You're the 25th smartarse to come in here this morning and say that," she replied. Okay, she didn't, but from her weak attempt at a smile she certainly wanted to.

I bought six of the things to keep me going for the rest of the day. Slightly over the top, but if Andre Agassi can pig out on bananas during breaks in his matches, then I was going to do likewise with Bakewell Puddings. Good for the potassium levels. Not.

I found a bench beside a mini-roundabout and sat down to eat a pudding and watch the world go by. After a couple of bites, I noticed two men standing close by, looking at me. The taller one had some severe-looking tattoos up his arms. As I continued eating, I overheard one of them say, "You go and ask him".

"Er, excuse me, but are you Gary Pallister?"

Now there are three things I should tell you about Gary Pallister:

1 he played football for Middlesbrough and Manchester United

2 apparently I bear a passing resemblance to him

3 this had happened before. Twice, actually...

The first time was in a bar in London, when a guy came up to me and said "Are you Gary Pallister?" The second was on a train from Kings Cross to Leeds, when a young boy accompanied by his father asked me for my autograph. I had to break his heart by saying that if he thought I was Gary Pallister, he was mistaken.

After the train incident, I swore that if it happened again, I would say that I was Gary Pallister. Unless it was a child asking, as it wouldn't seem right conning a little one.

So there I was in Bakewell, cornered by these two men in their forties, far too old to be going around asking people for their autograph. And the big man's words are hanging there in the air…

"Er, excuse me, are you Gary Pallister?"

"Yes, yes, I am," I said, doing a very poor attempt at Pallister's north-eastern accent.

"Can we have your autograph?"

"Of course you can. Who shall I make it out to?"

"Phil and Paul."

I signed 'To Phil and Paul, Best wishes, Gary Pallister.' Now I might have felt really bad about this whole scenario if it hadn't have been for one small point. They simply took the piece of paper I'd signed and walked off. No 'thank you' or 'cheers', 'good luck'. Nothing. It wasn't until the following day that I realised they had probably been Manchester City fans, intent on using it as bog roll.

Back at the car, I examined my map book. Once again, I'd veered massively off-course. If I continued in the direction I was heading, I'd end up in Manchester, missing Yorkshire altogether. To get back on track, I needed to follow the yellow line heading north-east across the page to Baslow, home to a pretty good tennis club according to Richard and Seb from the previous evening.

Despite having lived in the north of England for almost three years, this was my first visit to the Peak District. Why bother when you've got the Dales and the North Yorkshire Moors on your doorstep? Cruising over the hills, windows down, David Gray's *White Ladder* on the car stereo, I couldn't believe what I'd been missing. And the roads were empty. Were the tourists staying away after the previous year's foot and mouth crisis, or had the *Derbyshire Times* been running malicious reports on my imminent arrival?

Peak District residents are being warned to be on the lookout for a deranged man with receding hair carrying a bag of tennis rackets.

Police believe Spencer Vignes, 33, may be on a mission from God to bring the game of tennis to the masses.

His victims so far have included drug addicts, children, Koreans and Birmingham security guards.

Morris Minor-driving Vignes was last seen leaving Derby two days ago heading in the Matlock direction. He is prone to talking complete bollocks and may be under the impression he is Burt Lancaster, the late Hollywood movie-star.

A police spokesman added that Vignes was also wanted in questioning with the May 1st tennis ball attack on the All England Club at Wimbledon.

Baslow probably wouldn't warrant a mention on any map if it wasn't for the famous stately home on its doorstep. Chatsworth House is one of Britain's main tourist attractions north of London, a simply stunning building that makes Hampton Court Palace look like Didcot Power Station. It is owned and lived in by the Duke and Duchess of Devonshire, who employ around 500 staff to run the house and gardens, together with the 1000-acre park surrounding it, much of which was designed by Capability Brown, the Alan Titchmarsh of his time.

The house itself is loaded with more antiques than you can shake a stick at, including paintings by Rembrandt, a gallery of neo-classical sculptures, and a Rolls Royce jet engine (yeah, I couldn't work that one out either). Mary, Queen of Scots got to know the place quite well during the latter part of the 16th century, when her cousin Elizabeth I had her imprisoned there on several occasions. As they say, you can't choose your family. Still, if you're going to be locked up, it may as well be somewhere like Chatsworth.

A light drizzle had begun to fall by the time I reached the village. I found myself a B&B, signed the registration form in the name 'Mr Rodney Laver', one of the greatest tennis players of all time, and changed into some casual clothes to go for a walk around Chatsworth Park. Well, I wasn't going to find a court in the grounds of a stately home, was I?

Wrong. There it was, just about visible behind a line of trees close to the park's southern entrance. Half of me wished I hadn't seen it at all. Even travel writers are entitled to a break sometimes. I returned to the B&B, pulled on my tennis gear and drove back to where I'd found the court. Being on private land, I decided to do the right thing and drop in at the main office for the Chatsworth Estate to ask permission to play.

It took me about five minutes to explain all about my trip to the woman in the reception area. She referred me to someone else (another five minutes), who passed me on to someone else (ten minutes, as I think she was slightly deaf). I was about to give up altogether when a man in a suit appeared and introduced himself as Nick Wood. Nick was Chatsworth's Deputy Agent, second in command of everything on the estate besides the house, where the Duke and Duchess ruled the roost. And he was willing to have a couple of rallies with me. That was if he could find the key to the court.

"I swear it's around here somewhere, but we had some painters in earlier today, and they might have gone home with it."

Nick and I walked from room to room searching for the elusive key, him talking about the estate as we went.

"The leisure facilities here for the staff are quite excellent. We've got a golf club, a tennis club, a cricket club, a swimming pool and a gym, all for the use of employees and their families. The tennis club alone has about 100 members.

"But there's only one court!"

"I know. It can be a problem, but there is a booking system which works pretty well."

Providing you don't mind waiting four weeks for your turn to play. The key having done a disappearing act, Nick asked if I wouldn't mind returning the following morning for our rally. That would give him time to track it down. Not ideal, but I didn't really have any alternative.

Back in Baslow, I went in search of the tennis club, discovering it just up the road from the B&B. Good facilities for a small village, including three floodlit courts. Thursday, by a stroke of luck, was club night so there were plenty of people around to play. I fell in with Ron, Robert, Dave and Matthew, and the five of us played doubles all evening, taking it in turns to sit a set out.

By about 9.30, I was completely shattered and well up for a pint. Nick had told me Baslow boasted some excellent pubs, and I was eager to check them out with my new-found tennis mates. Just a couple of quick ones, you understand. No late-night lock-ins followed by shenanigans involving road cones and shopping trolleys. But they all had really interesting jigsaw puzzles to finish, or discussion programmes chaired by aggressive Scottish people to watch. So I was on my own again. I returned to the B&B to take a shower. Kicking my shorts off,

I realised I'd spent the evening going round with the remains of a Bakewell Pudding all over my arse. Little wonder nobody came drinking with me.

Rather than spend the rest of the evening in a bar with nobody to talk to, feeling like a fart in a space suit, I decided to check out the local Italian restaurant. The place was completely empty – never an encouraging sign, but at least I'd be able to call home on my mobile phone and talk very loudly without pissing people off.

Ever since Alex first learned she was pregnant, the two of us had struggled to agree on possible names for the little alien growing inside her. The reason for this lay in Alex's occupation. As a junior-school teacher, she has taught virtually every name under the sun, and grown to dislike a fair proportion of them. So we couldn't have Tom, because Toms whistle while the register is being taken. Sorry Sarah, you roll pencils backwards and forwards across the table during the silent-reading period. And so on.

Eventually we settled on Rhiannon for a girl (nice and Welsh, and the title of a great Fleetwood Mac song), but the boy still remained a problem. Walking through Chatsworth Park earlier that day, I'd done a bit of brainstorming. Before Alex went to bed that night, I wanted to see what she thought of my latest list.

"What about Greg?"

"No."

"Why not? Greg's your mate, good at sport, always there when you need him."

"Still no."

"Okay then. Ivan. Nobody would argue with someone called Ivan Vignes."

"Now you're being stupid."

"No I'm not! How about Bjorn."

"Why Bjorn?"

"Think about it. How many Bjorns have you heard of?

"Well, there's Bjorn Borg, and Bjorn whatshisname out of Abba…"

"Exactly. You've heard of two Bjorns, and they're both rich and famous. So it stands to reason our Bjorn might be too."

"He's not going to be called Bjorn. He'll be growing up in Yorkshire, not Stockholm. Give a child a name like that in Normanton, he'd never live to see five."

"Yannick?"

"Goodnight, love. Sweet dreams."

That night I lay awake well into the early hours with a cramping sensation in my right shoulder. I knew exactly what the problem was. The more tennis I played, the better my serving was getting. As a result, I was hitting the ball harder and faster, putting the muscles in my shoulder under increasing pressure.

Some number-cruncher once calculated that Goran Ivanisevic had served more than 10,000 aces during his career, many travelling at over 130 miles an hour. That's not including aces hit while he was a junior player, during training sessions or in friendly matches. Add on the several thousand other winning serves that opponents managed to touch with their racket, and you begin to see why the Croatian's left shoulder at one stage resembled a high-speed train crash.

Now I hadn't been counting the number of aces I'd hit since leaving Sussex, but I reckoned the figure probably stood at around 12. Yet there I was, wincing away and reaching for the painkillers I'd bought way back in Ruislip. Could have been worse, I suppose. At least the tennis elbow had kept a low profile for a fortnight.

The next morning I returned to the Chatsworth offices to meet Nick again, the pain in my shoulder having subsided overnight. He looked surprised to see me, and ever so slightly disappointed.

"You still want to play in this weather?" he asked, looking out of the nearest window at the columns of rain blowing in across the hills.

"I wouldn't be here otherwise. Did you find the key?"

Nick nodded. The painters had it all along. I handed him a racket and we walked out to the court, a fair percentage of which was underwater. Halfway through our short game, Nick got the giggles. He had clearly never played tennis in the rain dressed in a suit before, and seemed to be quite enjoying the absurdity of it all.

After four rallies, condemning one brand-new ball to a watery grave in the process, the heavens well and truly opened. We ran for cover. Back in the warm surroundings of the estate offices, I noticed Nick grinning at me and shaking his head.

"You think I'm mad, don't you?" I asked.

"Mad!" he barked. "I think you're completely crazy."

Postscript:

A few weeks later, I was at Wolverhampton races when I saw in my programme that a horse called Bakewell Tart was running in the 3.30. Having bored the friends I was with rigid telling them its name should actually be Bakewell Pudding, I sloped off to put a fiver on it to win. And it did, netting me £30. Proof, if ever it were needed, that a soft spot for rich food can pay.

CHAPTER TWELVE

Kylie

"For better or worse, the environment you are brought up in has an effect on you. Even if I was on the highest peak in the Andes, I would still be from Sheffield."

Jarvis Cocker

Things are going badly on court number four at Sheffield's Graves Tennis Centre. I'm 0–3 down and serving at 0–40. Lose this point, and the first set is as good as over. My serve lands in, but shorter than anticipated. I'm caught in no-man's land between the baseline and the net. Absolutely fatal. The ball flashes past me on my left-hand side, about a foot inside the line. Fuck it. For the first time on my journey, I'm being well and truly caned. And I feel powerless to do anything about it.

Oh, and my opponent is in a wheelchair.

I'm going to write that again, as weeks later I still can't get my head around what happened that afternoon. *My opponent is in a wheelchair.*

In 1989, when he was 28 years old, Kevin Plowman suffered a mountaineering accident that left him paralysed from the chest down. Life was put on hold amid a blur of hospital visits and the anxiety of adjusting to a new world without the use of his legs. Always a keen sportsman, he eventually took up table tennis, both as a way of meeting people and having something to do.

"While I was in hospital, I remember someone saying how disabled people could play wheelchair tennis. But at the time, it just wasn't an option in my head. I felt better suited for table tennis.

"Then, in 1993, I was playing down at Stoke Mandeville, and there was some kind of tennis exhibition-match also going on. I decided to have a go. Someone threw me a ball, I hit it back and immediately I thought 'This is for me.' It seemed to have the aggression and the adrenaline rush that table tennis just didn't have."

Kevin returned to his native Yorkshire, determined to give the sport a go. Slowly he began working his way up through the wheelchair tennis leagues, employing an able-bodied trainer to help him improve his game. The hard work seemed to have paid off when he was selected to play in an international tournament in Moscow. However, what should have been a dream come true turned into a nightmare.

"The tournament organisers ran off with all the money, and we ended up staying in army barracks with tank-tracks everywhere, which isn't good news if you're in a wheelchair.

"When I got back to Britain, I wasn't sure if I wanted to go through anything like that again. But Jayant Mistry, the top British player, told me it had been a one-off, and persuaded me to play in the next tournament in Israel. That went really well, and it just snowballed from there."

The high point of Kevin's career so far had come in 2001 when he was selected to play in a demonstration game of wheelchair doubles during Wimbledon fortnight. The match took place on a day when rain severely affected the order of play at the All England Club. The BBC, stuck for live footage, ended up showing recorded highlights of the wheelchair match throughout the afternoon.

"That was my finest day. I even got to serve the first ball of the match, making me the first wheelchair player ever to hit a ball at Wimbledon. Afterwards my girlfriend and I went to watch a bit of Tim Henman's semi-final against Goran Ivanisevic on the big screen, and we couldn't move for people asking to have their picture taken with me and sign their programmes. It was my five minutes of fame. I loved it.

"We'd been trying to get the All England Club to let us play on grass for years, but they just used to say it would damage the courts. I think we proved them wrong. Hopefully it won't just be a one-off thing, and will continue for years to come. The sport needs that kind of exposure."

For those of you wondering how the hell it works, the rules are exactly the same as normal tennis – with one exception. The ball is allowed to bounce twice rather than once. Kevin believes the similarities make tennis the perfect example of a sport that disabled and able-bodied people can play together. To demonstrate this, he challenged me to a match.

I have to admit I felt a degree of unease about this. Never having watched Kevin play before, I just couldn't see how it was going to work. I'm no Lleyton Hewitt, but I really believed I would be too strong for him. Surely the topspin on my serve alone would make the ball unplayable for someone in a wheelchair?

Kevin, on the other hand, had no such reservations. "Let's just see how it goes," he said as we took to the court, an indoor one with a smooth carpet surface.

Before starting, we agreed on two rule-changes. Kevin would be allowed a first and second serve, while I had to make do with just a first. And the ball could bounce twice on his side on the net, once on mine. I won the toss, elected to serve, and off we went.

At 0–2 down, I was still finding my feet, getting used to the one-serve rule and Kevin's flat returns. Being in a wheelchair, his shots were coming at me much lower than I was used to, to the point where

I was almost on my knees trying to hit the ball. By the time it got to 0–4, the whole thing was in danger of becoming a mismatch. Inside my head, Motorhead and the Manic Street Preachers had never sounded so off-key. All I could do was applaud Kevin and curse my pre-match arrogance.

I lost the first set 2–6, then went 1–3 down in the second. Kevin seemed able to anticipate my shots before I'd even played them, his every return landing within a foot of a tramline. My serves gradually got weaker and weaker. Those of them that managed to cross the net at all, that is.

Then I finally started using the mothballed organ known as my brain. My shots had been landing way too short, giving Kevin all the time in the world to adjust his position and blast the ball back at me. Midway through the second set, I started hitting them longer. The ploy worked. Kevin began struggling for room at the back of the court. His bullet-like returns made way for safer, defensive lobs, easy meat for a player such as myself who enjoys coming to the net.

From 1–3 down, I fought back to 6–5 up. Kevin squared it at 6–6 and we were into a tie-break. And ladies and gentleman, it was an epic. But one I still lost, blowing five set points in the process.

I should point out that a couple of hours before facing me, Kevin had played and won two tough sets against another wheelchair player. We are talking about a *seriously* fit man here.

"Sport is a great vehicle for any disabled person to regain their self-confidence and self-belief," said Kevin afterwards over a coffee at the tennis centre's snack bar. "When I first had my accident, sport was the last thing on my mind. I had so many other things that I had to come to terms with. But after a while it dawns on you that a big part of your life, and your social circle, has been removed. The only way back is to start competing at something again. My something was tennis."

It was impossible not to feel inspired by Kevin Plowman. Yet the sad reality was that up until his accident, tennis had been a closed door. Kevin had always seen it as a middle-class sport, not something a working-class Yorkshire lad should really be taking part in. His disability had broken down that barrier. The people he played against on the wheelchair circuit didn't care what job he had or car he drove. He played tennis, and that was good enough for them.

So that was the good news story on Day 23. Now prepare yourself for the bad news. Because it's time to be afraid for the future of British tennis. Very afraid.

That morning, I'd been driving down off the Derbyshire hills into Sheffield's southern suburbs when I saw a sign pointing to the Abbeydale Park Tennis Club & Academy. Expecting to find a couple of tatty nets and a wooden hut masquerading as a changing room, I was bowled over to discover a purpose-built tennis centre with 14 courts, including two indoors. I parked the Moggie and went inside to find someone to hit with.

The big chief was a man called John Gledden, a local tennis coach who had first come to work at Abbeydale in 1990. To cut a long story short, he liked the place so much that he bought it. Since then, the Academy had produced a number of promising junior players, while the adjoining tennis club had seen its membership grow to 600 players. John's ambition, according to a sign hanging in the posh reception area, was to "create tennis for everyone in Sheffield", whatever that meant.

I know, I know. Where's the bad news in that? Just bide your time. I'm building up to it.

I asked if I could speak with this John guy, and was told he was currently coaching his 11-year-old daughter, Annabel, on one of the indoor courts. But I was welcome to wait. From the players' balcony, I watched the two of them going through their practice drills. Annabel certainly hit the ball well, and it came as no surprise to learn that she was currently ranked third in England for her age group.

When the training session finished, an Academy employee took me onto the court to meet father and daughter. John was fascinated to hear about my journey, and invited me to hit with Annabel, who in four days time was off to Madrid to take part in a tournament. After a shaky start, I'm proud to say I more than held my own against the protégé. As our final rally built to a climax, I walloped an unsportsmanlike shot down the line for a clean winner. I had to do it, just in case she ever became famous. *Did I ever tell you about the time I left the great Annabel Gleddon for dead?*

Being a Friday morning during term-time, I had wondered why Annabel wasn't slaving away in chemistry rather than working on her forehand. I didn't have to wait long to find out.

"Last year, when Annabel was 10, we went to see the headmaster of the local secondary school we wanted to send her to," said John. "As she was showing such huge promise, we wanted to know if there was any way she could have time off from her lessons for coaching, and catch up with her academic work in the evenings at home.

"The head said that the only time Annabel could have off school would be during normal games lessons, which amounted to little more than two hours a week. Those are the rules laid down by the education authority, and there was nothing else the school could do to help. We understood that. But two hours just isn't enough. Not if she is going to make it as a professional player. So we approached a private school instead. They were willing to give her four mornings off a week to accommodate her tennis."

Which must cost a penny or two.

"It does, but we had no option. At least with me being her coach, we had already managed to save

196

some money. Nowadays, it costs between £23,000 and £25,000 per year to employ a coach to work with someone of Annabel's standard. Only the top five per cent of the population can afford that kind of money. Annabel's good. But, and I don't want to sound like I'm blowing my own trumpet here, she wouldn't be anything if I wasn't around to coach her. It would just cost too much."

This was beginning to get depressing. John's argument was this – that despite countless initiatives aimed at getting more British youngsters to play tennis, turning professional was only an option for those from wealthy backgrounds. I could see what he meant. Twenty-five grand plus private school tuition-fees equals more than I've earned in any single year since I was born. Whatever was growing inside Alex would have to make do with football or rugby. Sorry little one. No Wimbledon or Davis Cup for you. Not unless, to paraphrase The Clash, daddy became a bankrobber.

I asked John what he would do, given the responsibility of bringing British tennis up to scratch with the rest of the world.

"I would divide the country into areas, pick ten coaches for each one, and pay them £50,000 a year each. Then I'd tell them to go out, find the best young players, and coach them for free. That's what the Lawn Tennis Association should be doing.

"There are some great young players in this city, including many from the council estates and the poorer multi-ethnic areas. But the truth is that many of them don't stand a chance. That's down to money, and not being able to afford access to the right facilities. And it's the same in every town and city, right the way across the country. It's shameful."

I wished Annabel good luck in Madrid, and thanked John for his time. What he said appeared to confirm my worst suspicions – that Britain's attitude to tennis isn't really that different from 1984 when I was a kid. When the day goes down, it's still money that matters. The proof was out there in the clubs or the public parks. Where were the young guns I hoped I would see, gearing up to take over from Tim Henman and, er, Julie Pullin? Answer – using their precious spare time to play something else. Sure, I'd seen plenty of youngsters strutting their stuff on the country's courts. Unfortunately, the vast majority had been using them for football, netball or basketball, not tennis. And though many of the clubs I visited had boasted about their large junior memberships, I'd yet to see the evidence with my own eyes.

"You'll have a good time in Sheffield," John said as I dug around in my pockets searching for the keys to the Morris. "Plenty of clubs and public courts. Is that shoulder of yours okay?"

I lied. No amount of stretching or flexing seemed to take the stiffness away. I swallowed another painkiller, and went off to get hammered by Kevin Plowman.

That evening, I decided to splash out and book a room at the Etruria House Hotel in Sheffield's Broomhill district. Fifty quid a night and, being at the heart of the city's student population, food and drink on tap 24/7. I signed in as Jimmy Connors, and told the Clive Dunn spitting image in charge of reception I would be staying for two nights. Then my little joke backfired.

"Can you pay for the room in advance, please? House rules, I'm afraid."

Of course I couldn't. Not with £12 in my pocket and a credit card in the name of Spencer Vignes. It took me an hour on foot to find a cashpoint that was working and, with one Sheffield hill looking very much like another, I got lost on the way back. Served me right for having the cheek to impersonate the one and only Mr Connors.

Two nights in Sheffield seemed like a wise move, especially with all the shoulder gyp. Didn't want to be overdoing things. But before putting the Donnay away for the evening, I had a long-standing appointment to keep. As a man of my word, I was going to go in search of Weston Park, to see if the public courts Roger Taylor played on as a kid were still there. Either way, I would write back to the British Davis Cup captain and let him know. Clive Dunn had said it was only a ten-minute walk away, but suggested I go before dark as there were "lots of alcoholics and druggies about". Been there, done that on this trip.

I arrived at dusk just as the sun was setting, the plimsoll line of night steadily creeping up the steep west-facing hills of the city. The courts were still there, three of them, in pretty poor shape compared to the immaculately-kept park gardens. I set my stopwatch to 20 minutes and waited for the first passer-by. As I stood there, playing keepy-up with a ball on the head of my racket, a young blonde-haired man came and sat down on a bench about 20 yards from the courts. I looked at him. He looked at me. I put the racket down and began walking towards him, spiel at the ready. He got up and did likewise. It was as though he was expecting to see me.

"Hi there," I said.

"Hello. My name is Simon. Where would you like to go?"

"Pardon me?"

"Where would you like to go? Um, you are cruising, aren't you?"

"Eh?"

And then I realised what he meant. He had come to the park to pick up men. Oh my God, what was I going to do? He was, after all, the first person I'd seen. By my own rules, I had to ask him to hit a ball with me. Live and let live, but the chances of that happening after our cross-wired introduction were absolute zero.

"No, I'm here to play tennis. I'm sorry."

Without saying a word, he turned and disappeared into some bushes. I served one ball and packed my racket away, before an undercover cop jumped out of a tree and accused me of being tennis's answer to George Michael. I think Simon probably got what he wanted that night. On my way out of the park, I must have spotted a dozen single men lurking in the shadows (writing this some weeks later, I still haven't got round to contacting Roger Taylor with my Weston Park update. Perhaps you, dear reader, would be kind enough to do it for me. Just drop him a quick line saying his childhood tennis haunt is now Sheffield's gay pickup joint. Thanks. I owe you one).

Thinking back to the early eighties and my childhood growing up in Sussex, I have two clear memories of Sheffield. The first is of watching Arthur Scargill on the evening news, standing on a podium somewhere in the city addressing thousands of miners at the beginning of the 1984/85 strike. It may as well have been taking place on Mars. Everyone looked so radical and passionate, qualities not regularly associated with Sussex folk, many of whom would probably struggle to even spell the words.

The second was a TV drama called *Threads* in which Sheffield got nuked by the Russians. Shown when Reagan and whoever happened to be in charge at the Kremlin that week seemed hell bent on annihilating the world, it scared the pants off everyone my age. Except that is for kids growing up in Sheffield, who all got parts in it as extras. Since moving north, I've met three people who all thought it was a great laugh to be vaporised as schoolkids by those evil Commie bastards.

Walking through the city centre on a Saturday morning, 18 years after the mushroom cloud went up, the town planners seem to have done a pretty good job of rebuilding. But the radical, passionate nature of the people remains. The high street is packed with protest groups and charities all competing for cash and signatures on their petitions. First up was a woman raising money for a local mental health group, to whom I gave 50p. Next came a gaggle of people campaigning against experiments on animals, in particular cats and rabbits (good cause, and worth £2 of my hard-earned cash plus a signature). They were followed by four guys fighting privatisation of the Post Office (a £1 donation to help with publicity costs), who were standing shoulder to shoulder with a couple of ladies from a children's hospital (a £2 coin, which was all I had left in my pocket).

Then came the grand finale. A whole army of Socialist Worker bods, armed with megaphones, all shouting slogans in unison. Couldn't understand a word any of them were saying. I asked one, a young guy looking about as depressed and emaciated as Morrissey circa 1985, what was going on.

"We don't want asylum seekers scapegoated."

For what?

"Everything. New Labour is scapegoating them to deflect away from their own failings, playing on people's fears of job insecurity and housing problems. You've only got to look at the way the media have covered the problems encountered by the asylum seekers living in Dover."

"But that's down to the media, isn't it, not the government?"

"That's what you think, citizen, but..."

I'm sure what came next was extremely interesting, but I'd never been called 'citizen' before, not even during my student days at a fairly lefty polytechnic. I wanted to laugh. But the poor kid so believed in what he was saying, I didn't want to insult him. I signed his petition.

"Thank you, citizen."

No bother, comrade. By the time I'd reached the bottom end of the High Street, I felt like setting up my own little action group. Something to do with collecting signatures supporting the beheading of all the old farts at the Old England Club and the Lawn Tennis Association, replacing them with a sort of Duma to make and enforce tennis law. I'd call myself the 'Socialist Tennis Worker', dedicated to getting normal kids from Portsmouth to Perth winning Grand Slam tournaments by 2010. Or I could find the nearest cash point, go and have a coffee and spot a few look-a-likes. Who would have guessed that Al Pacino, Tina Turner and Leo Sayer all spend their Saturday lunchtimes in Henry's Bar on Cambridge Street?

Browsing through a copy of the *Sheffield Telegraph*, I came across a story regarding the reissue on video of a short film called *City On The Move*. COTM was made in 1972 to promote the image of 'swinging Sheffield', talking up its industrial importance, the fact it had more retail stores than any city north of London, and that Bob Monkhouse regularly played at the Fiesta Ballroom on Friday nights. There's a good chance you may even have seen *COTM*, or at least part of it. Remember the beginning of *The Full Monty*, which featured some archive footage of Sheffield set to a very BBC World Service type narration? Well that was the opening few minutes of *COTM*, the team behind *The Full Monty* having paid £400 for the privilege of using it.

Back at the hotel, I dug out a book I'd brought with me featuring heaps of facts and figures about films and actors made and born in Britain. *The Full Monty* had two pages devoted to it, including the map of a 'Full Monty Walk' around Sheffield taking in many of the locations used in the film. Sounded like fun. I could take my rackets and look out for tennis courts along the way.

Over the next couple of hours, I came across the school where Tom Wilkinson failed his job interview after being distracted by a garden gnome, the Langsett Road filling station where young Nathan attempted to talk Robert Carlyle out of doing the strip, and the lane where Steve Huison tried to commit suicide in his car.

By the time I reached Sheffield's Hillsborough district, I reckoned I'd done enough walking, my intended destination of the Shiregreen Working Men's Club (where the guys performed the final strip) still miles away. I bought a can of fizzy drink and sat on a bench in Hillsborough Park, keeping an eye on the deserted public courts about 100 yards away. In the distance, Sheffield Wednesday's football ground towered over the surrounding streets like the giant mothership from *Close Encounters of the Third Kind*. For the second time on my trip, I'd unintentionally stumbled across somewhere forever linked with death. I may have forgotten all about Kegworth, but the events of 15th April 1989 – the day 96 people lost their lives at an FA Cup semi-final between Liverpool and Nottingham Forest – will stay with me until my dying day. Ask any football supporter over 30 years of age where they were that afternoon, and they'll be able to tell you straight away. It's our Kennedy moment.

After a few minutes, three thirty-something guys arrived and started knocking up on the park courts. Excellent. One spare doubles-place for me. I went over and introduced myself. They were all members of Hillsborough Tennis Club, which used the park courts for fixtures against other teams. That afternoon, they had arranged to play a league match against Hallam Grange, who were due to arrive at any minute. However, one of Hillsborough's players hadn't turned up yet, and his teammates were beginning to get jittery.

This was it. The moment I'd been waiting for. A tennis club in desperate need of help. They were going to ask me to step into the void, and I was going to win in straight sets without losing a point to become the toast of Hillsborough. Oh happy day.

I began knocking up with the team captain, a man by the name of Stevie Splash. "It's not my real name. I run a nightclub in Bradford, where I do a bit of DJing. Stevie Splash is my DJ name. It's what all the lads call me."

Eager to impress, I went through the whole repertoire – backhands, forehands, overheads, volleys, and a couple of serves for good measure. The opposition arrived, but still Mr Splash didn't ask me to play.

And then the missing man arrived. Wearing only one contact lens. The other one had gone AWOL somewhere between his home and the park. Surely they weren't going to let him play? It would be like handing Hallam Grange the points before a ball had even been hit.

"Thanks for the knock, mate," said Mr Splash. "Good luck with yer book."

Led up the aisle only to be ruthlessly dumped at the altar. Bastards. I returned to my bench and watched One-eyed Man warm up by hitting balls into the foot of the net. It wasn't long before Mr McEnroe came to join me.

"You're never gonna get a game you know. No-one likes you. They think you're weird.

Anyway, I thought your shoulder was playing up?"

"Not now John."

"Yes, now. And remember. It's Mr McEnroe to you. You know something? I've been watching you over the last few weeks, and you're not half the player you think you are. Make that a quarter. You lost to a guy in a wheelchair, for Christ's sake! Even that drug addict had you on the ropes. Face it. You're not one of us. Just go home."

"I'm not listening."

"Asshole. I won Wimbledon three times. I won the US Open four times. I've got 70 other career titles. You lose out on a place in some poxy park side to a guy who can't even see. Jerk."

I fell asleep on the bus taking me back towards the city centre, and woke up somewhere in the southern suburbs. I stumbled to the front and asked the driver where we were.

"Where is it you're going?" he replied.

"The city centre."

"That was about four miles back. Get off here at this stop, walk across the dual carriageway and catch any bus going back the way we've come. They all go to the city centre."

"Thanks very much, but where are we?"

The folding doors had already closed and the bus was pulling away. An elderly lady who had got off at the same stop informed me I was in Norton. As suburbs go, it didn't look too bad. Nothing like Birmingham's Ladywood or Winson Green. So I decided to walk and scout for courts. It wasn't long before I discovered a row of them in Graves Park. As I arrived, a group of lads in their late teens/early twenties were just leaving. I asked if any them wanted a quick knock. One did, a guy called Paul wearing a New York Yankees tracksuit top. We hit for a few minutes, and then played a set, which I won 6–3. One set became two. And again I won 6–3. Your loss, Hillsborough.

Afterwards, Paul asked me if I'd like to join him and some student friends later at a pub in the city centre called the Red House. With nothing better to do, I accepted. We agreed to meet again at 9pm, and went our separate ways to shower and have a bite to eat.

When I arrived, there was no sign whatsoever of Paul. I bought myself a pint and stood at the bar on my own. Across the crowded room, a portly bloke with a guitar was belting out Bob Dylan's *It's All Over Now, Baby Blue*. He was good. Better than the real thing if you ask me. At least you could understand the words, which is more than can be said for Bob's delivery.

He finished to enthusiastic applause, and was replaced on the small stage by youngish man with a goatee beard, who made a complete hash of another Dylan song, *Subterranean Homesick Blues*. But it didn't matter, as everyone helped him through. Heads back, drinks raised, throats cleared. All together now.

'YOU DON'T NEED A WEATHERMAN TO KNOW WHICH WAY THE WIND BLOWS!'

After listening to five different Dylan songs, all performed with varying degrees of success in South Yorkshire accents, I asked the middle-aged woman stood beside me what the occasion was.

"It's *Dylan Night!*"

"What's *Dylan Night?*"

"It happens every year in here, on the nearest Saturday to his birthday. Everyone gathers to sing Dylan songs. It started a few years back, when he was due to play in Sheffield and cancelled at the last minute. A few of us got together and decided to have a concert anyway. Anyone can get up and sing. Why don't you have a go?"

I mumbled something about not knowing the words to any Dylan songs besides *It's All Over Now, Baby Blue*, and that one had been sung already.

"That doesn't matter. You can do it again. Just get up there, and we'll all sing along with you."

Opportunity well and truly knocked for Spencer Vignes – and he bottled it. Salvation came with a tap on the shoulder. It was Paul. He apologised for being late, and introduced me to Matt, Ruth, Laura and Polly, his friends from Sheffield University. Polly was quite simply drop-dead gorgeous, and she knew it. To the point of being rude. The kind of girl that behaves like a Hollywood movie queen, even though she has never been further west than

Hounslow. I bought them all a round of drinks. Not even so much as a 'Thank you' from Polly for her Bloody Mary. Should've spiked it to the eyeballs with a little help from the water blister on the inside of my right toe.

Paul's friends – Polly aside – were nice enough people, but the age gap of at least a dozen years meant I only understood a fraction of everything they said all evening. I was the outsider, the one unable to pepper his speech with references to trendy Sheffield nightspots and groovy student-union people. At one stage, I did find something in common with Matt and Ruth. They were both originally from Sussex, and spent much of their late teens hanging out at the same clubs and bars in Brighton as I once had. However, they were all now known by different names, which made me feel even more of a dinosaur.

By 10pm, I'd had enough of the Dylan covers and Matt telling me he knew somebody who knew somebody else whose best friend's dog had done some building work at Fat Boy Slim's apartment. Hands were shaken and Ruth gave me an affectionate peck on the cheek. I was making for the door when I felt a tug on the sleeve of my coat. It was Polly, the girl who up until then hadn't bothered to say a word to me all night.

"I hear you're writing a book. You won't forget to put me in it, will you?"

No Polly, I won't. So here goes. You're a self-centred little madam with the manners of a chimp that has just discovered there's no bananas for tea. There. That ought to do it.

I barely slept that night. Nothing to do with mad shagging in the next room or fear of mushroom clouds. No, it was something far worse. Besides my right shoulder stiffening up once again after the match against Paul, the tennis elbow seemed to have returned. Within the space of an hour, the slight twinge I'd felt while filling the kettle in my room had become a dull, yet constant ache. Painkiller time again. 1am became 2am became 3am. I lay there watching *Barbarella* on TV, trying to ignore the McEnroe voice and concentrate instead on the miracle cure of Jane Fonda's breasts. They seemed to work wonders, and I fell into the deepest of sleeps, waking up the following afternoon to discover I'd missed check-out by the small matter of four hours. I dressed and hurried down to reception. My embarrassment was offset by the look on Clive Dunn's face. He clearly thought Mr Connors had already checked out. I paid up front for another night, giving my elbow an extra day's rest away from the courts, and he fixed me a late breakfast.

Afterwards, I tried to reach my physio at his home to get some advice about the elbow. I had a pretty good idea he would say at least one of two things. Either:

a) stop playing now, or

b) that I should've stopped way back in Wycombe, like he'd advised me to, thus preventing the risk of permanent damage.

After half an hour of the engaged tone, I gave up.

"Havin' trouble getting through?" asked the bearded Scotsman sitting opposite me in the lounge reading *The Observer*.

Despite wanting nothing more than to go back to bed, I started telling him all about the elbow and my trip. He was in Sheffield visiting his daughter, who was studying at the university. And he was a retired doctor.

"Ye shouldn'ae be puttin' it under soooo much pressure, not if it's givin' ye grief. And ye need to go easy on those painkillers. Take a couple of days off the tennis, then see how it feels. Dinae push yerself, ye hear?"

I heard. Despite being only an hour's drive down the M1 from Normanton, I didn't want to jeopardise my journey, especially having come so far. I went back to see Clive and reserved my room for the Monday night as well, then went to find some ice from one of the many local pubs to wrap around the elbow.

I spent the best part of the next 36 hours back in Henry's Bar catching up with my travel notes, reading the papers, clocking the occasional look-a-like. Paul Gascoigne, Cher, Roger Daltrey, Dylan Thomas. One waif of a lass accompanied by a couple of burly hunks really might have been Kylie Minogue. In Sheffield city centre, on a Monday lunchtime? I should be so lucky.

By Tuesday morning, having managed to wake up at a reasonable hour and with the elbow feeling okay, the time felt right for moving on.

"Have you enjoyed your stay in Sheffield, Mr Connors?" asked Clive as I checked out. Despite the elbow, my encounter in the park with Simon, and the misery of being overlooked in favour of the one-eyed man, I had.

"Would you like a hand with your bags?" Before I could answer, he had scooped up the one containing my rackets and was heading towards the Morris.

"That's funny. I hadn't realised until now. You've got the same name as a famous tennis player, haven't you?"

I could see the cogs turning inside his head. Clive had been taken for a ride, and he knew it. Give the man credit. He chose not to say anything, though if the roles had been reversed, the words 'You wanker' wouldn't have been far from my lips.

I drove out of Sheffield on the Penistone Road, stopping to fill the Morris up with petrol in Hillsborough, just down the road from where One-eyed Man had ruined my Saturday afternoon. As I stood in line waiting to pay the cashier, I caught sight of Kylie Minogue again. Only this time she was looking out at me from the front page of the local Star newspaper. The little minx had been in town performing at the Sheffield Arena. Of course – the burly hunks had probably been minders. I should've asked her for a quick, erm, knock up. Kylie is, after all, a big fan of the game. A few years ago she even recreated that memorable seventies poster, the one with the female tennis player lifting her skirt to reveal a bare bottom, for a magazine photo shoot.

Yeah. Kylie and me playing in Weston Park on a hot summer afternoon, with her in that short skirt. That would be enough to turn Simon straight.

CHAPTER THIRTEEN

Jungleland

"I think I learned more going round the clubs in Barnsley than I learned at Oxford about the human race in general."
William Hague

It's the final Saturday in May, and I'm standing on a court just outside Penistone, allegedly the highest market town in England (that's altitude, not dope-consumption). Today, it certainly feels like it. Rain clouds are sweeping in across the Pennines from the west, lining up like World War II bombers to dump their loads on the people of this weathered place. The wind is so strong I'm squinting to prevent my contact lenses being whisked off to Sweden. Any second now, a twister is going to pitch down out of the dark sky and start vacuuming *everything* up. Because in Penistone, where the northern tip of Derbyshire meets Yorkshire meets the heavens, there's absolutely nowhere to hide.

Please God, someone walk past in the next nine minutes and 35 seconds, otherwise I think I'm going to die here. A passer-by will find my decomposing body in a few days time, once the storm has passed. The post-mortem verdict will be death by hailstones the size of buses. But, according to the write-up in the *South Yorkshire Times*, 'at least he died with a tennis racket in his hands'.

There's a flash of lightning over the hills towards Manchester. I count the seconds to the rumble of thunder. Ten. That's okay. Far enough away for me not to have to worry about being turned into pork scratchings. I walk to the side of the court bordering a road. No cars or pedestrians in sight. It's been like this ever since I arrived.

Five minutes and three seconds to go now, and I'm in a race against time with the rain clouds, which are almost directly over me. Suddenly a car appears. It slows and turns into the driveway of a nearby house. A man gets out and starts unloading shopping. I approach him, introduce myself and do the spiel. His name is John Hamilton, and despite the conditions he's willing to have a knock. Albeit a very quick one.

We stand either side of the net, within touching distance of the cord, and gently pat the ball backwards and forwards. During our second rally, the clouds begin to drop their payloads. There's another flash of lighting. Five seconds. The thunder is now more of a crack than a roll. John is already halfway back to his house. I follow him, and we shelter together under his porch watching the horizontal rain being blown from west to east.

"It can be bleak up here, especially during the winter, but you get used to it after a while," he says. "When the snows come, the roads west of here are always the first in the country to close. The Woodhead Pass seems to spend more time shut than it does open. But it's a beautiful place. Why did you decide to come to Penistone?"

I told him it was the luck of the draw, and I was making up my route as I went along.

"Well, meeting you makes a pleasant change from the kind of normal people you get around here, that's for sure."

'A pleasant change from the kind of *normal* people you get around here.' I think he meant it as a compliment, as in I was doing something different with my life, and that made me an interesting person to meet. But sitting in the Morris in the rain, 31 days, 334 miles and 141 courts after leaving Warnham, John's words had set off a few alarm bells. Of course I wanted to be an interesting person. Doesn't everyone? Yet with my decadent twenties well behind me, and fatherhood looming, I was beginning to think that being *normal* wouldn't be such a bad thing. I was missing out on a vital stage of our baby's development, because most *normal* men wouldn't go off and do what I was doing when their other halves were pregnant.

Which begged the question: why was I living out of B&Bs and a Morris Minor when I should be at home decorating the nursery, going to ante-natal classes, or helping Alex battle with her morning sickness?

Act One, Scene One

A father and son are driving home together after watching Brighton and Hove Albion thrash Arsenal 4–0. It's been a great afternoon, the kind that bonds a father and son forever. At school, the son is currently learning all about how babies are made. He wants to find out more about what his parents were doing with their lives while he was still wriggling around inside his mummy.

Son: Daddy. What were you doing when mummy first felt me kicking inside her?

Dad: Playing tennis in Penistone, son, playing tennis in Penistone.

Son: Wow! What about when I was old enough to first hear noises outside mummy's body?

Dad: Um, let me think now. Probably in Sheffield, being overlooked in favour of a one-eyed man for a place in Hillsborough's squad to face Hallam Grange.

Son: What about when I first started pulling faces and sucking on my fingers?

Dad: Oh, I know that one. Oxford, trying to break into Tim Henman's parents' place.

Son: You are my daddy, aren't you?

Director's note:
No such conversation has ever taken place in the history of father/son relationships, but why let that get in the way of some marvellous dialogue and a serious case of screenwriter's paranoia?

I called Alex and went all melodramatic on her. I told her I loved her, that I thought of her always, that I'd do anything for her and the little one when it was born, including buying them both convertible MGs and doing all the washing-up for the next 18 years.

"Have you been drinking?"

"No, I just felt I needed to say a few things, that's all."

"Look, the nursery can wait until you get back. You know I'm not even suffering from morning sickness. And the ante-natal classes don't begin for another two weeks, and you'll be back by then, won't you?"

"Of course I will." I looked down at the problem elbow and crossed my fingers.

There's a school of thought about Yorkshire that suggests the further north you go, the more beautiful the scenery becomes. And I'm sorry, all you proud South Yorkshire folk, but I've got to admit I agree with it. How many people do you know who take their holidays among the railway sidings of Doncaster, or the scrap yards of Rotherham? Nope, everyone heads for the dales or the moors of North Yorkshire, to places like Robin Hood Bay, Settle, Scarborough and Harrogate. That said, South Yorkshire does have a few picturesque bits tucked away, including stretches of the journey north from Sheffield to Penistone. Lord knows I had enough time to appreciate them because, thanks to my deteriorating physical condition, it ended up taking me four days to complete a drive that would normally last around half-an-hour.

At first I thought the two-day break from tennis in Sheffield had done the trick. I came across several courts on the Tuesday while working my way through the city's northern suburbs, and neither the elbow nor the shoulder gave me any problems. When a lad in his twenties, called James, challenged me to a match at Thorncliffe Tennis Club, I didn't think twice.

James was obviously a fairly good player – good forehand, sneaky around the net, slice rather than power on the backhand. But on the day he met me, his serve just went to pieces. Double fault followed double fault, to the point where I began to feel sorry for him. I remembered reading something about a Brazilian tennis player called Maria de Amorin, who served 17 double faults in a row while playing a match at Wimbledon in 1957. I wasn't counting, but I do know this – during our two sets, I won three whole games without even hitting a ball.

It was agony to watch. Yet James refused to moan, and continued to play some fantastic shots on my serve, winning enough points to make it a contest. He must have worked me pretty hard, because during the closing stages of my 6–2 6–4 victory, the elbow began to hurt again.

I checked into a pub providing accommodation just off the A61 south of Stocksbridge, and raided the freezer in the bar for more ice. Within a couple of hours, the shoulder ache had also returned, together with a pain in the bottom of my right foot, presumably some kind of strain resulting from weeks of bouncing around on my toes. Despite what the retired Scottish doctor had said in Sheffield, I went back on the painkillers.

And there I stayed for the next two nights without hitting a ball. The temptation to drive home to Normanton, rest for a few days, and then return to pick up from where I'd left off was huge. But that would've been against the spirit of the trip. So I read, wrote and went for a couple of short walks over the surrounding hills, trying to conserve my dwindling cash reserves by avoiding the bar altogether. Which takes an incredible amount of will power, especially when happy hour lasts from five to nine-thirty.

I decided to give my body another go on the Thursday, travelling on to Stocksbridge where I hit a few test serves on the deserted courts at the local tennis club. The shoulder said yes, the elbow and foot said no. Two more nights recuperating in a B&B on the outskirts of town. Nice farmhouse this time. Three cats, two dogs, chickens galore, hardly saw the owners after I'd checked in. Bliss. Could've walked around all day in the buff without anyone noticing – and probably would have done if I were Brad Pitt: Movie Hunk, instead of Spencer Vignes: Receding Nobody. Went into Stocksbridge on Friday and bought a snazzy-looking elbow support at the chemist's in the high street, then sat in the garden all afternoon drinking lemon squash and reading a book by William Goldman, the genius who wrote the screenplay to *Butch Cassidy And The Sundance Kid*. Suddenly, being an injured sportsman didn't seem so bad after all.

During the Stocksbridge lay-off, I began to wonder what life would have been like had I become a professional tennis player. Would I have turned into one of those pain-in-the-arse athletes permanently sidelined by injuries? Some friends of mine support Tottenham Hotspur, a football club with a player called Darren Anderton on its books. You may have heard of him. A few years ago, these friends (along with a fair percentage of other

Tottenham fans) started referring to Anderton as 'Sicknote', a dig at the amount of time he seemed to spend on the treatment table at White Hart Lane.

Would I have been tennis's answer to the unfortunate Anderton, derided by followers of the game the world over?

The answer had to be yes and no. Yes, I'd have been an injury-plagued son of a bitch. No, because I wouldn't have been around long enough to be given a nickname. While football players can rely on an annual wage to keep them afloat while injured, tennis players aren't so lucky. No play = no pay = no money to travel the globe competing in tournaments. A serious injury can mean retirement and having to get a real job. So I'd have become the fastest-serving supermarket shelf-stacker in West Yorkshire.

By Saturday I was ready to try again. Elbow support in place, I hit the lanes heading over the western edge of the Pennines between Stocksbridge and Penistone. Lots of big properties with plenty of land, the kind likely to have private courts secreted away behind rows of poplars. Eventually I caught sight of one in the grounds of a wonderful three-storey house that had clearly been added to over the years, turning it from some kind of shepherd's cottage into Balmoral. I parked the Morris in a lay-by and walked up the drive, racket at the ready. No sign of life, despite a BMW parked outside. After leaning on the doorbell for the best part of five minutes, it was decision time. Should I walk straight back to the Morris, or go via the court in the far corner of the garden and hit a serve?

It would've been rude not to, eh?

And then all hell let loose. No sooner had I reached the mesh fence surrounding the court than a dog suddenly appeared, announcing its arrival with two short barks. I couldn't tell you the breed, but it was large, ran extremely quickly and didn't like having me around. I shut the gate to the court, saving my neck but trapping myself from the outside world.

We stood and looked at each other for what seemed like an eternity, but was probably only a couple of minutes. It barked again, yet still nobody came out of the house to see what all the commotion was about. Either it was wild, or simply left to roam free while the occupants were out. This was terrible, potentially worse than Mr Pisshead in Birmingham. He had been three sheets to the wind. This thing was fit, sober and hungry. For me.

I edged closer to the mesh and tried talking to it, much as I would to my cat at home. All high-pitched, soppy tones containing lots of friendly 'Hellos', emphatic 'Good Boys' and 'Aren't You Lovely's? Amazingly, it worked. The beast fell to the floor and started rolling about on the grass, paws in the air. I took a ball from my bag and started bouncing it. It jumped to its feet again, ready to play. I had found my way out.

I held the ball high up above my head. Its eyes followed the trajectory of my arm expectantly. I repeated this process three times, just to check its attention was now fixed on the ball and not me. And then I walloped it, as hard and as far away from me as possible. Rover took off like a champion greyhound across the lawn. I opened the gate and ran like nothing on earth in the opposite direction towards the Morris. I didn't look back, so I can't tell you if it did a U-turn and came after me. All I can say is this. Fear can make the human body go like an express train. And if you want proof, look out for the scorch marks on the soles of my tennis shoes.

After Penistone, it was time to consult the map again. Manchester seemed to be cropping up on too many signposts for comfort. I had to make sure I stayed on the right-hand side of the Pennines, even if the prospect of a night out in the city that gave us New Order and Boddingtons seemed appealing. However, a map only comes in handy if you know where you are to start with, which I didn't. I drove on another couple of miles until I came to a signpost at a T-junction – right for Barnsley, left for Huddersfield. I turned right.

I'd hate to be a Barnsley native, and not because I think it's a horrible place. Far from it. Coming from Barnsley would mean having to put up with the rest of England, particularly national newspaper reporters, cracking a constant stream of patronising jokes at your expense. All of which stopped being funny in 1949. Even the Leeds media portray Barnsley folk as cloth-cap wearing, brass-band playing, parkin-eating inbreds, unemployed since the last of the mines shut down.

Try these for size:

Barnsley Put-down Number One: When local author Joanne Harris had her bestselling novel *Chocolat* published, each review concluded with words to the effect of 'a work of art, especially when you consider the downtrodden, miserable, God-forsaken place she comes from'. Or something like that.

Barnsley Put-down Number Two: Whenever a football team gets promoted to the marble halls of the English Premier League from the lower divisions, national newspapers seem legally bound to run the line '...no more trips to Barnsley on a rainy Tuesday night' on their back pages. The joke backfired when Barnsley Football Club was promoted to the Premier League in 1997. However, after losing 0–6 to Chelsea, 0–7 to Manchester United, 0–5 to Arsenal and 1–4 against both Wimbledon and Southampton during the opening weeks of the season, it wasn't long before the mocking began again. 'The Tykes' were relegated back into obscurity after just one year.

Barnsley Put-down Number Three: During the spring of 2002, Barnsley planners unveiled their ideas to reinvent the town in the style of a Tuscan hill village, with more greenery, restaurants and Italian-esque buildings. The laughter from news desks the length of England could be heard in Florence.

I'll conclude my rant on behalf of the people of Barnsley by saying this. Taking the piss out of what Dickie Bird once referred to as "the greatest little place in the world" from behind a word processor in Battersea is one thing. Next time, why not try it at half-past eleven on a Friday night in Market Street. See what reaction you get then (note to the Mayor of Barnsley – I'll expect a cheque in the post for public relations services rendered by Friday).

I cruised into town and found a B&B in Dodworth Road. Thirty-four pound fifty for a room in an attic with no fire escape. I couldn't be bothered to look for anywhere else, so it had to do. I dumped my bags in the Death Trap and went exploring, Bruce Springsteen's *Jungleland* on the car radio as I drove round the one-way system by the Town Hall. If Bruce had been British, he'd have come from a place like Barnsley; as working-class as it gets, but where people look on the bright side of life, no matter what. His album titles might have been a little different though: *Greetings From Dearne Valley Park, Born In South Yorkshire, The Wild The Innocent* and *The Shambles Street Shuffle*.

In the Wilthorpe area of town, I came across Barnsley Tennis Club; four courts, all floodlit, great-looking clubhouse, nobody around to play.

Which was surprising, as the day had brightened up considerably since Penistone. I set the stopwatch running and tried the clubhouse door. It was locked. A sign stuck to a window gave a name and a number for people to ring if they were interested in becoming members. I called and spoke to Dominic, the club secretary. He took my details and promised to call back if he could find anyone who fancied a knock.

I stood on the clubhouse veranda, humming the tune to *Jungleland* and watching the trains plying up and down the valley below the courts. After 20 minutes, I was all set to take one serve and move on when my phone rang.

"Hello," said the voice at the other end. "You don't know me, but my name is Shane O'Keefe. I'm the men's team captain at Barnsley Tennis Club. Dominic tells me you're after a game."

"Yes, yes I am."

"How good are you?"

"I'm average, I suppose. No great shakes. I've only just started playing again after a bit of a lay-off."

"Would you be available to play in a league match for us tomorrow?"

And at that moment, I loved Barnsley and everything about it. At long last, I'd found a club who wanted me. It was as though my whole trip had been building up to that moment. I was ecstatic, and couldn't say 'Yes' fast enough.

"What ranking are you?"

"I beg your pardon?"

"Never mind. We'll worry about that tomorrow. The match is at home against the David Lloyd Club from Hull. If you can, get down there for about 1.30 – that'll give us time to sort out your guest membership. See you then."

I had planned on hitting the town that evening to check out the Barnsley nightlife. No chance of that happening now. Since Shane's call, I had slipped into athlete mode. I wasn't going to touch a drop of alcohol all evening. Barnsley versus Hull in the National County League might sound like small potatoes to you, but to me it was all four Grand Slam tournaments rolled into one. I had to be up for it.

It was only after returning to the B&B that I realised I still had over 18 hours to kill until the match. That's a lot of time in a town where the main form of Saturday-night entertainment involves pubs, clubs, curry houses and Chinese restaurants – all on my banned list, together with anywhere else that could possibly make me ill for the following day. Playing tennis was also out as I didn't want to aggravate the elbow/shoulder/foot/all of the above, and risk jeopardising my moment of glory.

That left me with a toss up between *The Eurovision Song Contest* and *The Guns Of Navarone* on TV. I nipped down to the local supermarket, bought some sandwiches, a couple of bananas and a chocolate bar, and was back in my room in time to see Cyprus get things underway in Tallin. By the fifth entry (Spain, in case you're really bothered), the Euro-pop novelty had well and truly worn off. So *Navarone* took over. Shame on me in the first place for overlooking Gregory Peck and David Niven in favour of The United Colours of Sweaty Middle Aged Men In Spandex.

I woke the next morning to a familiar sound outside – rain. As though it hadn't pissed down enough during the past five weeks. Obviously somebody up there had screwed up on my rain quota for the year. Or just didn't like me. So much for going to church back in Warnham.

I pulled back the curtain. Grey, grey and grey as far as the eye could see. This wasn't part of the plan. Today was meant to be about blue skies, nice temperatures, the lightest of breezes to cool you down without playing havoc with the serving action. It was almost nine o'clock – five hours for the Gods to cut me some slack. Otherwise, with Normanton and journey's end edging ever closer, the odds would be well against me ever getting to play for a club.

After breakfast, I checked out and went to the one place in town that served coffee on a Sunday morning – McDonald's. I know, I know, but it was either that or sitting in a shelter at the bus station. And it gave me the chance to catch up with some writing. Every few minutes, I glanced outside to see if it had stopped raining. If anything, it was getting heavier. Around midday, the twister that had been stalking me since Penistone finally touched down. The drains immediately began to overflow, turning the streets outside into streams. People stopped eating to gawp at what was going on outside. There was a flash of lightning, followed almost immediately by a bang of atomic proportions. The windows shook. A woman screamed. Kids started crying, and burglar alarms everywhere burst into life. If a 200-foot-high wall of water had loomed into view and smashed into us, like something out of *The Poseidon Adventure*, I wouldn't have been surprised.

Then it stopped, almost as suddenly as it had started. The grey skies parted and blue patches appeared. The sun came out, the streams stopped running and everyone carried on eating as though nothing had happened. Apart from one panic-stricken child, who wasn't going to stop freaking out until he'd brought the whole place down. It looked like my prayers had been answered. I returned to the Morris to play Vince's tape and get my head together. This was it. I was going to slog my guts out in the name of anyone who ever had anything to do with Barnsley – Brian Glover, Arthur Scargill, Dickie Bird, Darren Gough, Bruce Springsteen – everyone apart from Michael Parkinson, who has always struck me as a little too clever for his own good. I was going to do them proud. Barnsley 'til I die.

I arrived back at the tennis club bang on one-thirty. Shane and the other members of the team had beaten me to it, and were already warming up. I was introduced, sworn in as a guest member and told I was playing as the fourth seed. In other words, I would be up against their number four.

"Just do your best and enjoy yourself," said Shane, picking up on my nerves. "You'll be fine. Did you say you had a ranking?"

"No. Does that matter?"

"Not really. All competitive club players get a ranking according to the number of games they play. The more you win, the higher you are ranked. I'll make something up for you."

I wondered if that was within the rules. Not wanting to talk my way out of playing, I kept my mouth shut and went over to shake hands with the Hull players, who had just arrived in a fleet of cars. All of them looked dead sporty and serious. They clearly hadn't driven eighty-odd miles across northern England to make up the numbers.

My opponent was a guy called John Fuller, considerably shorter than me (always a disadvantage in tennis) but without an ounce of fat on his body. He looked mean, not dissimilar to the sinister cyborg robot in *The Terminator*. I knew straightaway that this wasn't going to be the kind of match where the two of you share jokes in between points. He was out for a no-nonsense, straight-sets win. There would be no smiling, not even if I ran for a ball, missed it, hurdled the net, ploughed through a fence and ended up face down in a pile of cow crap.

I wrapped my bandana around my forehead, pulled the elbow support on, picked up my racket and walked onto Court Four. John went through some pre-match stretches and joined me for the warm up. Ten minutes of backhands, forehands, overheads, volleys and serves. I seemed to be hitting the ball okay, despite my nerves. I felt confident.

"You ready?" asked John.

"Ready as I'll ever be," I replied.

We stood at the net and tossed a coin to decide who would serve first. I called heads, won, and gambled by choosing to receive, hoping to catch him cold and gain an early break. No such luck. I won the first point, but he won the game.

We changed ends. I had to win my first service game. The Manics and Motorhead had started to sound a little stale in my head over the past fortnight. So I decided to ditch *Faster* and *Ace Of Spades* in favour of *Jungleland*. I stood on the baseline, put the needle on the record playing in my head, fast-forwarded through the intro to the bit where Bruce's guitar crashes in, threw the ball in the air and served. And two forehands later, I'd won the point. By the end of the song, I'd won the game. It was 1–1. I was doing okay.

A voice in my head told me not to get too excited. All that old crap about it being a marathon, not a sprint. Then I won the next two points on John's serve, and got completely carried away. The words 'Game, set and match Vignes' began ringing in my ears. I was going to get a letter of apology from the Sussex Lawn Tennis Association, begging forgiveness for their shoddy treatment of such an outstanding talent back in the early eighties. The All England Club would invite me to sit in the Royal Box on Men's Finals Day at Wimbledon – and I would refuse. And Bruce Springsteen would send me a guitar, inscribed with the words 'To my good friend Spencer, you did it in *Jungleland*, Best wishes, The Boss'.

By the time I came to my senses, I'd lost not only that game but also the following two. I was winning plenty of points, just not the ones that really mattered. For example, three times in that first set, it got to Advantage Vignes. Yet instead of going for the kill, I sat back, hoping he would make a mistake. And on each occasion, he punished me.

I lost the set 1–6. This time I had no-one to blame except myself. The elbow, shoulder and foot were all behaving themselves. I'd played some good shots. But, according to John McEnroe, I wasn't focused enough.

"Not very good on the big points, are we?"

"No, John, I know."

"*And your head is in la-la land. Get a grip. Fast. Otherwise you're gonna be outta here. Remember me in 1981 against Borg at Wimbledon? I fought for every ball. I chased lost causes. I NEVER switched off.*"

"What are you saying?"

"*Are you listening to me. I'm saying DON'T SWITCH OFF, JERK!*"

"Okay."

"*Now go out there and show me what you're really made of. He's half your size. You should be at the net, dominating play, using your height as an advantage. You can make pancakes out of this guy.*"

"I will, John, I will."

"*You mean 'I will, Mr McEnroe, I will'.*"

"Whatever you say."

We were playing a best-of-three-sets match, so I had some catching up to do. Again I kept on getting him to deuce, or advantage, only to let the big points slip away. The difference in our fitness levels also began to show. Though my aching body was holding together, I just couldn't compete with John. Afterwards, I discovered he was a policeman who kept fit by playing either squash or tennis every day. If I'd known that beforehand, I think I'd have stayed in McDonald's.

I tried my hardest, but it wasn't good enough. I lost the second set 6–2. We shook hands and went to watch the remainder of one of the other matches in progress. I'd achieved my wish of playing for a club in a competitive fixture. But it had come at a price. Now I knew I was nothing more than a very average player. Then again, put your racket down for 17 years and what do you expect?

Final result: Barnsley 2 Hull 2 (or so I thought), our second seed having also lost his match. With several hours of daylight left, I wanted to press on before bedding down for the night. While the Hull captain was safely out of earshot, I cornered Shane to thank him for fielding a very grateful ringer in his squad.

"That's fine. You gave it your best shot. Maybe you can do better in the doubles."

"Doubles?"

"Yeah. You and Mark are playing against their number two and three."

Oh, right then. It looked like I was going to be staying in Barnsley longer than planned. I called the B&B in town and reserved my old room for another night, then went to meet my partner, who bore an uncanny resemblance to the Wimbledon getaway driver. Would the elbow hold up for at least another two sets? For Mark's sake, I certainly hoped so.

This might sound like an obvious thing to say, but I'm going to say it anyway – there is a huge difference between playing doubles and singles tennis. Singles is a game where you alone are responsible for doing the business on court. Doubles, on the other hand, is a team effort where a degree of telepathy with your partner is vital. The right arm has to know what the left is doing, and vice versa. Otherwise you look like fools.

During our first set, Mark and I showed about as much telepathy as the captain and navigator on the Titanic. We chased after the same balls, stood on the same side of the court, left shots for each other, and lost 0–6. It was a textbook example of how not to play doubles, the icing on the cake coming when one of Mark's serves hit me right between the shoulder blades. I'm surprised our opponents didn't die of laughter.

But in the second set, Mark and I began to click. We turned a 1–3 deficit into a 4–3 lead, before Hull squared things at 4–4. In the next game, at 40–30 to us, Mark missed an absolute sitter of a volley at the net. It affected his concentration badly. Instead of going 5–4 up, we went 4–5 down. They duly won their service game to take the set and win the match.

Shane and his doubles partner won their match to make it Barnsley 3 Hull 3. But Mark remained disconsolate.

"We should've had that set. We were on top. That has to be the worst fucking shot I've played in years."

I came out with the usual stuff to try and make him feel better – you had too much time, it could happen to anyone, blah blah blah. But the truth was I was glad he'd netted the thing, sparing us from a third deciding set. The elbow support had given me some peace of mind while playing, but I'd felt a slight twinge during the penultimate game. Within half-an-hour of finishing, my shoulder had also seized up.

I was now only a day or two at most away from Normanton and the end of the road. The thought of going completely lame with the finishing line in sight didn't bear thinking about.

CHAPTER FOURTEEN

The Prince

"Don't go down the pits, lad."
Miner Fred Ferry's fatherly advice to his future rock
star son, Bryan

Ned Merill is almost home. He has achieved his
dream of swimming through every private and
public pool separating a friend's house from his
place. But what began on the opposite side of the
county as an adventure has steadily turned into a
nightmare. Two years seem to be missing from his
life. We are never told where Ned has been during
this time but, judging from his fragile state of mind,
a stay in prison or a psychiatric hospital seems a
safe bet. People he once regarded as friends now
insult him to his face. We learn that he was in debt,
his daughters hated him, that he had a mistress.
Someone who started out as a likeable character
has been shown up to be a complete shit.

Yet we are left feeling sorry for him because of the following, final scene.

An exhausted Ned, still wearing only his swimming trunks, has reached the front gate to his home. It is covered with rust. He forces it open and begins walking up a path through an overgrown garden. There's a clap of thunder, and it begins to rain. He pauses beside the remains of a tennis court. Inside his head, he hears his children laughing as they hit a ball backwards and forwards. The sound fades.

He continues up the path until he reaches the front door to the house. It is locked. The rain is now falling harder. Desperate to get inside, he starts pounding the door. The camera pans left to a broken window. Inside we can see that the house is empty and derelict. Either the wife and daughters that Ned has talked about throughout the film are dead or they deserted him a long time ago. Inconsolable, he breaks down and collapses to the ground. The picture freezes, and the credits roll.

Thankfully, getting wet at various stages on our travels appeared to be the only thing that Ned, Burt Lancaster's character in *The Swimmer*, and I had in common. Alex hadn't left me, my house wasn't falling down, and I had more clothes to choose from than a flimsy pair of black swimming trunks.

So why was I feeling so utterly fed up? Well, for starters there was my complete mess of a body. You know all about the elbow and shoulder. Now my right foot was beginning to give me serious grief. In the space of five days, it had gone from being a minor irritation to a constant source of pain. On top of that my right hand, the one I'd injured playing football the previous year, was starting to play up. Come the end of each day, I was finding it increasingly difficult to straighten the fingers, a legacy of having them wrapped them around a tennis racket and steering wheel for the best part of five weeks. They seemed to be stuck in a permanent, claw-like grip. Like a bad special effect from a Hammer House of Horror film.

But the aches and pains were nothing compared to what occurred on the morning of Day 33. In hindsight, I was surprised it hadn't happened already. Launching into a big serve on a park court in the village of Darton, the strings on my beloved Donnay racket finally gave up the ghost. They'd carried me all this way, only to break with less than 20 miles to go until Normanton. I was gutted (very funny, I know, but I was!). According to the *Yellow Pages*, tennis-racket restringers hadn't yet colonised the former pit villages dotted along the border splitting South and West Yorkshire. So out came the first reserve, something black and shiny called a Prince Outrage, to take over for the remainder of the trip.

Not everything was doom and gloom though. How could it be when you're seeing the world from behind the wheel of a Morris Minor? Three hundred and fifty miles after leaving Warnham and Mogs/Moggie/RAA 954G – call her what you will – continued to go like a dream. I couldn't recall a single morning when she hadn't started first time, which considering the amount of rain we'd encountered had to be a miracle – albeit a minor one (all right, all right, enough of the crap puns). It was almost as though she was enjoying a new lease of life, having done little apart from potter around Normanton for the previous three years. So what if the driver's side door-handle had come off in my hand in Derby? We're talking about an old lady here. Sooner or later, the odd limb is bound to start finding its way loose.

Besides the death of my Donnay, Darton also threw up what had to be the most excruciatingly boring tennis match of all time, let alone my trip. My opponent was a tall, thin man, probably in his early forties, who I'm going to call Malcolm. Now I know I've already criticised travel writers who mock people for the pettiest of gripes. But in Malcolm's case, I hope the harsh words I am about to say about him will:

a) help him improve his style of play, which in turn will

b) prevent his opponents from wanting to beat the living daylights out of him for his unbelievably negative tactics.

Malcolm had a way of playing that involved putting snow on the ball. Almost every shot he hit had to go 50 feet into the air before landing on my side of the court. At first I thought he was having a laugh, but after a couple of games of this mind-numbing, neck-aching tedium, I began to realise it was his one and only shot. He'd obviously tried it once, found it to be quite effective, and carried on using it ever since.

It certainly worked against me. Malcolm's game plan meant I was reduced to playing overhead smashes, or waiting for the ball to bounce ten feet into the air before striking it (giving me enough time to make a cup of tea, read *War and Peace*, and be back in time to hit the ball). I had *too much* time to think about where to place my returns, and began making mistakes. Should I put it to his backhand, forehand, do a drop volley, try and smash it up his arse? Oh shit, I've buried it in the net again.

"Fancy another one?" he'd said cheerfully at the end of the first set. No, Malcolm, I didn't. Things to do, people to see, you know how it is. Oh yeah, can you take a bit of constructive criticism? I'd rather share a court with Muffin the Mule than you any day. Learn to play properly, you freak.

The Malcolm Experience left me feeling slightly shell-shocked. I'd heard of tennis players using spoiling tactics before – McEnroe's tantrums, Boris Becker's coughing fits – but he had taken it to another plane entirely. It reminded me of the scene from Monty Python's *Life of Brian*, the one where the slave is sent out into a Roman amphitheatre to face a gladiator. But instead of fighting, the slave runs around in circles until the gladiator suffers a heart attack, and dies.

With my neck muscles crying out for a well-deserved rest, I stopped for lunch at The Spread Eagle in the village of Wragby, south-west of Wakefield. Nice pub, good atmosphere, packed with tourists in the area to see Nostell Priory, home to a huge collection of Chippendale furniture. I ordered some steak and kidney pie and sat down with a pint and a broadsheet in one of the few spare seats available. You could tell a man had decided what went in the paper that day. It was full of stories containing lists – Top Ten most expensive areas to live in Britain, Top Ten cheapest areas to live in Britain, top 20 most eligible bachelors in Europe, that sort of thing. A Ralph Harrison paradise.

However, two lists in particular caught my eye. One carried the names of the Top Ten male tennis players in the world that week, all of whom I'd heard of but who were by no stretch of the imagination household names. The other was yet another of those laughable *Greatest Films Ever Made* surveys, the kind that starts with *Citizen Kane* at number one and then degenerates into a roll call of obscure European and far eastern licks: *Pather Panchali, Andrei Rublev, L'awentura, Rasomon.* As for *Ugetsu Monogatari*, I thought he was a Japanese Formula One driver.

Where were *Get Carter, The Ladykillers, Ferris Bueller's Day Off, GoodFellas, Casablanca, Withnail And I, The Usual Suspects, When Harry Met Sally*? You know, normal films. Try as I might, I couldn't recall the last time I'd heard someone say:

"Excellent, *Au Hasard Balthazar* is on BBC2 tonight!"

I looked over at the group of four well-dressed, middle-aged people eating at the table next to me, and found myself wondering this – if I plonked the list of top ten male tennis players in front of them, would they react to it in the same way as I had to the film survey? In other words, how many of the ten would they be able to name? I'd been eaves-dropping on their conversation, and they seemed like nice people. So I introduced myself and set them the challenge.

Just in case you're bothered, the Top Ten read like this:

1 Lleyton Hewitt (Australia)
2 Gustavo Kuerton (Brazil)
3 Juan Carlos Ferrero (Spain)
4 Yevgeny Kafelnikov (Russia)
5 Tim Henman (Great Britain)
6 Marat Safin (Russia)
7 Tommy Haas (Germany)
8 Thomas Johansson (Sweden)
9 Andre Agassi (USA)
10 Sebastien Grojean (France)

The four managed to score a pretty poor two out of ten between them. Well done for Henman and Agassi; big fat raspberries for Michael Chang, Pete Sampras, Greg Rusedski and Goran Ivanisevic.

"Now if you'd asked me that 25 years ago, I'd have been able to tell you the lot," said Barry, visiting Yorkshire with his wife Linda and their friends Brian and Maggie from back home in Somerset. "Borg, McEnroe, Connors, Gerulaitis, Lendl, Nastase. We even went to Wimbledon a couple times, didn't we, love?"

Tongue-tied with a mouth full of shepherd's pie, Linda nodded.

"And it rained on and off both days, although we did get to see Arthur Ashe and... and... who was the fella with the big serve?"

"Roscoe Tanner?"

"That's him. I think it was the year he played Borg in the final."

I was impressed. Barry knew his stuff. I bought them all a round of drinks as a thank you for taking part in my quiz. Then Brian came up with an interesting point.

"Do you think anyone would have heard of Greg Rusedski if he was still a Canadian?"

And the answer, we all agreed, was no. He'd be nothing but another faceless new age player unable to hold a candle to anyone from the golden era of the seventies and early eighties.

"Wasn't his mother from Yorkshire?" asked Barry.

He was right. Greg Rusedski's mum had come from Ossett near Wakefield, a few miles from where we were sitting. She had been born in Dewsbury Maternity Unit, and emigrated to Canada in her late teens where she met and married a man from the Ukraine.

I told them a story I'd heard dating back to when Greg first became a British citizen in 1995. Desperate to trace his family roots, he returned to West Yorkshire at the invitation of the *Dewsbury Reporter* newspaper, who gave him a framed copy of his mother's birth certificate together with a picture of the town centre. The local council even threw a civic reception in his honour. Apparently, Greg had told a local journalist that he considered Dewsbury to be 'his second home'.

"I bet he's got a third and fourth by now, what with all the money he's earned," joked Brian.

"Has he ever been back?" asked Maggie.

I hadn't a clue, and told her so.

"Perhaps he'll return when he stops playing. He could buy Nostell Priory!" she added.

"No, he wouldn't do that. He supports Arsenal, so he'd want to stay in London," replied Brian.

"It is possible to survive somewhere without football," snapped Maggie.

Brian rolled his eyes. We were straying into dangerous territory, all because of some wacko conversation over Greg Rusedski's retirement plans. It was Linda, the epitome of calm, who stepped in to divert the conversation as far away from football as possible.

"Did you know that both Greg and Tim Henman are married to girls called Lucy?"

Brian said nothing, Barry kept eating, Maggie acknowledged the fact with a polite "Really?" It was time to leave.

I wished them all a safe journey back to Somerset, and returned to the Morris.

Back in 1984, you would've got better odds on me going to Mars than moving to West Yorkshire. The north–south divide seemed wider than ever. The south had work, money and was full of optimism. The north was on strike, broke and dejected. And they hated us for it – you could see it in their eyes when you went up there to watch football matches. I was convinced that one day Northern Man, tired of being pushed around once too often, would march south to steal our women, drink our beer, take our jobs and give everyone a darned good kicking (starting with Margaret Thatcher and working their way down to me). And I can't say I'd have blamed them.

After leaving Sussex in 1988, I did my best to live absolutely everywhere but the north – Cornwall, London, Berkshire, Melbourne, Cardiff, three separate spells in the USA. Until one night at a party in Hampshire, I met Alex. She was a

Yorkshire lass, and had grown up around Pontefract, the most Welsh-sounding non-Welsh place in the world. We married, moved to London, spent vast fortunes in rent on a two-bedroom flat. Well, one and a box-room built for a pigmy.

Despite a tidy joint monthly income, it wasn't long before we realised that staying in London would mean dying broke having never been able to afford to have kids. So we decided to move to either Cardiff or somewhere around Pontefract, to save money and be closer to at least one side of the family. Pontefract won when Alex was offered a good job teaching at a local school. Any quibbles I had about becoming an adopted northerner soon disappeared when we found a five-bedroom, three-storey house for sale in nearby Normanton for £85,000, less than the Pigmy Flat had been valued at earlier the same year.

How times have changed. Now it's the north that seems to have plenty of work, money and optimism, while the south sinks into a bottomless pool of debt created by the increasing cost of living. And a pint up here costs not much more than it did in Warnham in 1988. Now I understand why my father preferred to drink at home.

On a strip of land sandwiched between Pontefract's Prince of Wales colliery and the racecourse lie four public tennis courts. A man I know in Wakefield says he remembers how striking miners used to gather on them during the 1984/85 dispute, before crossing Park Road to picket outside the colliery gates. 'The Prince', as it's affectionately known to locals, is West Yorkshire's last remaining pit. Sorry, wrong tense. That should read 'was' West Yorkshire's last remaining pit, because a matter of weeks after my journey took me through Pontefract, it shut down. In its heyday during the late seventies and early eighties, The Prince employed more than 1,300 miners and produced over 1.3 million tonnes of coal a year. Many of those men are still part of the local economy today, having retrained as policeman, electricians, train drivers, journalists, priests, you name it.

On moving north, I fully expected to find a lingering bitterness among the mining communities over the way the industry was treated, and for the destruction of a way of life going back generations. Opinions vary from village to village, town to town, but this much I have come to understand – it was the cold, ruthless way in which many of the mines were shut that really stirred things up. Thousands of men were left on the scrap heap to fend for themselves, often without any warning. They were joined on the dole by countless others working in industries associated with mining, such as machinery manufacturing. Starved of money, many local shops, pubs and leisure facilities were forced to close. People were angry. Years later, people are still angry.

Yet say it quietly, but the actual mines themselves aren't missed. The air is cleaner, people are healthier, and the majority of the slagheaps that once scarred the landscape lie buried beneath green fields. Shopping centres, nature reserves, boating lakes and even dry ski slopes now stand on many an old pit site.

Perhaps 'The Prince' could be turned into a tennis centre, because there clearly isn't enough space to accommodate everyone who wants to play on the courts opposite the pit entrance. I drew up to find 24 youngsters, either in or not long out of their school years, running about with rackets. Only five were dressed in what could be described as sports clothes. The rest were in jeans, Doc Martens, Ben Shermans, anything clean that happened to be hanging up in the wardrobe that afternoon. The place resembled some kind of sixth-form fashion parade.

Every time I drive along Park Road, I turn to look at these courts. And on each occasion they seem to be busy. Even in the winter. Exactly why remains a mystery. The lines have faded, the nets are ripped to shreds, and the tarmac is in a worse state than Beirut High Street circa 1983. The only theory I can come up with is this. Where else is it possible to play tennis in full view of a power station, a pit, a racecourse and a football ground, all the while... GETTING HIGH OFF THE SMELL OF LIQUORICE WAFTING FROM THE NEARBY HARIBO SWEET FACTORY? Sweet-toothed tennis players the world over, this is your Mecca.

I approached a gang of male youths standing around two Peugeot 306s parked beside the courts. Dance music blared from two large rectangular speakers carefully positioned across the back shelves of each car. The youths were there to look cool, to pose, and certainly not to play tennis. But they'd been the first people I'd seen while parking the car, so I had to ask one of them to join me for a knock. Incredibly, Lee, group spokesman and owner of one of the Peugeots, liked my spiel and agreed to have a hit. He obviously carried a bit of clout in these parts, because as we walked onto the nearest court the six kids who were already playing there parted for us like the Red Sea.

Lee was fibbing when he said he'd never played tennis before. His shots were just too good for a complete novice. But in these parts, tennis isn't the trendiest of sports for men in their late teens – not like cricket, rugby league or football – so I won't fault him for trying to cover his tracks. We hit for a good quarter of an hour, the displaced six patiently watching from the tramlines, waiting to reclaim the court. As we played, I asked Lee for his thoughts on the pluses and minuses of living in Pontefract.

"Well, you got Kiko's I suppose (the local night-club), the KFC (Kentucky Fried Chicken – I think he's joking about this, but can't be sure), and some good pubs. Ponty's meant to have more pubs per square mile in its town centre than any other in the country, summat like that. But it's not really as good as Wakey. That's where me and me mates go most of time. There's more to do there."

I should say here that people in this corner of West Yorkshire abbreviate the hell out of everything. So Wakefield, Castleford, Featherstone, Pontefract and Normanton become Wakey, Cas, Fev, Ponty and Normy. If my name was Darren and I had a sister called Karen, we'd be known as Daz and Kaz. Recently, I have noticed one or two people calling me 'Spen'. In another couple of years, they'll have got it down to 'Sp'.

So what did Lee think about The Prince closing down?

"As long as it's not the KFC that's shutting, I'm not really bothered," he said, completely straight-faced. Fair point, I suppose (now I knew he hadn't been joking about it being one of Ponty's party hotspots).

Alex tells me there are kids at her school who don't know what mines are. Most children under the age of 16 in West Yorkshire have probably never even seen a working one. There's no shame in that. The pits belong to another time. It would be like asking a child of the seventies or eighties what they thought about the demise of steam trains on Britain's railways, or Accrington Stanley folding.

Lee returned to his mates, and I sat down on a patch of grass to make a phone call. I was now only two miles from home. After 33 days and 147 courts in different locations, only the public ones in

Normanton's Haw Hill Park remained (unless somebody had built one in a hurry while I'd been away).

"Hey love, it's me."

"Where are you?"

"Pontefract. I should be in Normanton in about ten minutes. Are you ready?"

"Do I have to?"

"Yes, you have to."

"Okay then. See you in ten minutes. But you owe me dinner somewhere nice for this."

CHAPTER FIFTEEN

'Normy'

**"Nothing can compare with the arrival of your
first child. Not even winning Wimbledon.
After all, tennis is only a game."**
Tim Henman

Normanton. There's something in its steely name
that tells you this is no quaint Cotswold hideaway,
or Cornish fishing village, in the same way that
Chipping Camden or Porthleven could never be
associated with coal dust and pit wheels.
Normanton is a proper noun not to be messed with.
He'll be your friend, but cross him and you'll live to
regret it, buried alive with gunshot wounds in the
gaps where your knees used to be. It's the Reggie
Kray on any map of England, bettered only by the
Ronnie Kray that is Gravesend.

Normanton owes its existence to the coming of
the railways during the middle third of the 19th
century. With lines converging on it from London,

Hull, York, Manchester and Carlisle, it became the Clapham Junction of the north. As buffet cars hadn't yet been invented, all trains stopped at Normanton for passengers to take tea and refreshments, served by girls in high-necked black dresses and white frilly aprons. Gladstone, Disraeli, Queen Victoria, at least two American presidents, even Dom Pedro, the Emperor of Brazil – they all came to Normy.

Then someone discovered coal in the area, and things really went ballistic. Thousands poured in to find work at the many pits that sprang up around the town. The colliery owners had rows of terraces built in which to house them; some poor quality, others not so poor quality (today, a mining survey is still part and parcel of buying a home in Normanton, to ensure it's not about to fall into an abandoned hole in the ground). With the pits came schools, libraries and more railways to cope with the coal trains. Boom time had arrived.

In 1905 it was decided that all these people needed somewhere central in which to chill out. A ten-acre plot was landscaped surrounding an area known locally as Haw Hill, which historians believe used to be the site of a Norman settlement (hence Normanton, or 'Noroman Tun', meaning 'Farmstead of the Normans'). Haw Hill Park came equipped with two bowling greens, tennis courts, a lake and a bandstand. Every Sunday evening, people would come out in their hundreds to sit and listen to musicians playing. Reading about it today, it all sounds like something from the animated seventies kids' TV programme *Chigley*, where each episode ended with the workers streaming out of the biscuit factory in time for the 'Six O'Clock Dance'.

Normanton is almost unrecognisable now from those days. The railway yards and the mines are long gone, and the station buildings in which world leaders once dined have been demolished. But Haw Hill Park remains the same. The lake, the bandstand and the bowling greens are all still there. So too are the three tennis courts. They're not used much, but that's partly down to the local council, which only bothers putting the nets up during the school summer holidays. For 46 weeks a year, you're more likely to find kids pulling 'wheelies' on them than practising hard to become the next Lleyton Hewitt or Serena Williams.

I guided the Morris through the tight little terraced streets of north Normanton and onto Ash Gap Lane, the road that runs beside the courts. And there was Alex, sitting waiting for me in the one car we own that's modern enough to boast hazard lights and power steering. Neither of us have ever been big on public shows of affection, but 33 days apart seemed a good enough reason to break with tradition. Plenty of hugs, kisses and 'You're looking wells', despite the fact I felt like death. Alex reckoned I'd lost a few pounds around the waistline and seemed leaner (despite the conveyor belt of cooked breakfasts I'd had along the way). She, on the other hand, had definitely gained a stone, possibly two. Legitimately, of course. Whatever was inside her bump was also very much awake.

So it was, standing beside the tennis courts in Normanton's Haw Hill Park, that I felt our baby kick for the first time. A truly wonderful moment, designed to melt even the hardest of male hearts. And I thought being walloped by Kevin Plowman in his wheelchair had been a humbling experience.

"Right then, let's get this over and done with," she said. "You got a spare racket?"

There were two reasons why, at short notice, I'd asked Alex to be my final victim. One, it's always nice to have someone there to greet you at the end of a long journey. Two, I knew that on a drab, rainy evening like that, there probably wouldn't be a soul around to challenge. I didn't want it all to end with one lonely serve on a deserted court. Alex hates sport – absolutely detests it. But she agreed to a couple of rallies partly to keep me happy and, just maybe, because she had missed me.

I handed her a Slazenger and we walked onto the courts, unswept since the previous summer and in desperate need of some TLC. It's not every day you see a woman-with-child playing tennis, especially one with a bump as large as Alex's. Melanie Molitor, mother of Martina Hingis and herself a former professional, once won a tournament while she was carrying the future

Wimbledon champion. But that had been during the very early stages of her pregnancy. It's probably a good thing that the park was deserted. I've heard Normanton's social services come down pretty hard on husbands who force their expectant wives into playing racket games.

We rallied across a non-existent net for a couple of minutes, me gently hitting the ball as close to Alex as possible to avoid her having to run. And then it was all over. I took a black marker pen from my pocket, the one I'd used to scribble my message to the All England Club, and wrote 'The Server – 148' on the ball, a reference to the number of courts I'd managed to play on. I left it sitting there in the middle of one of the service boxes, a DIY monument to five weeks of fun, pain, sweat and (look out, here comes the hippy bit) self-discovery. When I walked past again three days later, it had gone. I'd like to think the ball was discovered by a small child, and that it will inspire them to become the Bjorn Borg or Chris Evert of his or her generation. But deep down, I know it's probably being carried round Haw Hill Park in a dog's mouth.

I was home, and not even the sight of a small mountain of junk mail covering the mantlepiece in the hall could dampen my spirits. I'd only been away five weeks – a drop in the ocean compared to the average Russian cosmonaut – yet it felt a good deal longer. Walking from room to room, I couldn't decide what to do first; have a long soak in the bath, share a moment or two with the cat, run upstairs and crash out for half an hour on a proper double bed, one with a decent mattress made this side of the Cold War. In the end, I decided to pour myself a large glass of red wine and sit outside in the fading light with Alex, *Metro Music* by Martha and the Muffins playing through the open patio door. Forget about unpacking the Morris, checking my e-mails, and decorating the nursery. All that could wait until tomorrow. I just wanted to sit, talk and drink. Staring at my wife's stomach, it was only too easy to remember that in a couple of months' time, such things would be luxuries. As Maggie the Tamworth mum had said, "You won't find time enough to sleep, let alone play tennis."

Epilogue

It took me a long time to recover both physically and mentally from a trip that had spanned 14 counties, 365 miles and more serves, volleys and smashes than I cared to remember. It was weeks before I finally shook the habit of looking for courts while out driving. If I had a pound for every time I slammed on the brakes having spotted one, nearly causing a major pileup in the process, I'd be a wealthy man.

The pain in my shoulder and right foot subsided after a few days rest. The elbow took a week or two longer to recover, but at least there didn't seem to be any permanent damage. Unfortunately my hand, the one injured in the football accident, wasn't so lucky. At some point over the next few months, I'll have to undergo another operation to replace bone in my little finger worn away by sheer tennis overkill. And after that, there'll be yet more months of physio to deal with.

What did I learn on my journey? I know that Morris Minors were built to last, that my wife is a very tolerant woman, and that my ancestry could well be French. I've realised the voice that nags away at me whenever life's glass seems half-empty belongs to John McEnroe. I know that next time I walk through a suburb of Birmingham, I'll hire some bodyguards to protect me. And I know I'll never return to Weston Park in Sheffield when the shadows are starting to lengthen.

I know that when it comes to tennis, as with most sports, there is no substitute for actually going out and playing it. And I know that Goran Ivanisevic could have Chris de Burgh in a fight.

Unfortunately, I've also come to the conclusion that in today's Britain, talent alone just isn't enough for those who dream of becoming professional tennis players. The system demands you need money to succeed. Buckets of it. *But why?* It's not as though tennis is like motor racing, or power boating, where a million in the bank might just cover the cost of turning an ignition key. Far from it. Tennis should be one of the easiest and cheapest sports there is to take up. A racket, a couple of balls, an opponent or a wall with a net cord chalked across it, and you're away. That in mind, how come it's only those from comfortably-off backgrounds that ever get the opportunity to make a living from playing the game?

A couple of days after returning to Normanton, I called my old friend Steve Jenkins to see if he'd recovered from our match in Warnham.

"Did you make it then?"

"Yep. A few aches and pains along the way, and I got asked into some bushes by a man in Sheffield, but I'm home."

"You got what?"

"I got asked into some bushes by a man in Sheffield."

"Was he after what I think he was after?"

"Oh yes."

"What did you say to him?"

"I said, 'Only if you beat me in a best-of-three-sets match'. What do you think I said?"

"Bloody hell. So did your game improve after Warnham?"

"I think so. Hard to tell. When I was good, I was good, but when I was bad…"

"You were crap."

"No. I was worse than crap. Have you played again since?"

"I have actually, yeah."

This surprised me. It emerged that within a week of our match, Steve had gone out and bought himself a new racket. He was now playing regularly again with a group of people at work. A decade and a half after following me down the road to premature retirement, he had launched an official comeback.

"Perhaps we should make this rematch stuff an annual thing," I said. "You know, as a way of keeping fit and staying in touch."

"Good idea. You gonna beat me next time then?"

"Of course. Straight sets, no bother. You wait and see."

Fired by the challenge, I started looking round the Normanton area for tennis clubs. I'd always planned on joining one once the journey was over, determined to carry on playing having worked so hard to get back in shape. I contacted two clubs, the West Yorkshire in Wakefield and Riccall near Selby, and left messages for the membership secretaries to get back to me. Neither of them bothered. When I called the West Yorkshire's clubhouse again a few weeks later saying I wanted to join, a woman told me it wouldn't be worth it "because the courts are gonna have houses built on them soon."

"Can I leave my name and number anyway, in case someone wants to play a one-off game in the next week or two?"

"No love, you can't. I'm really busy at the moment and I haven't got a pen handy. Can you call back another time?"

With that attitude, why bother?

So, for the time being, I'm clubless. The Donnay sits in the corner of my office, its strings still broken. I haven't hit a ball now in four months. With every packet of crisps, bar of chocolate and Chinese takeaway I eat, my game slowly ebbs away.

And here's the twist. While I was away travelling, a brand spanking new swimming pool opened in Normanton. All mod cons, including lanes wide enough to accommodate a Boeing 747. You'll find me there most lunchtimes in my snazzy goggles, scattering grannies left, right and centre as

I plough up and down. I have, to all intents and purposes, become The Swimmer.

One day, I'll get the Donnay restrung, find a club that wants me and start playing competitively again. I'll become tennis's answer to Paul Newman in *The Hustler*, cruising the courts of northern England looking for action. 'Fast Spencer Vignes', they'll call me, the mean-looking guy with the sledgehammer serve. And a 1969 Morris Minor. One day.

Postscript

Rhiannon Mary Vignes was born by caesarean section in Pontefract General Hospital on October 1st 2002, weighing eight pounds and five ounces. At the time of writing, she shows no sign whatsoever of being interested in tennis, having slept through radio and television coverage of both semi-finals and the final of the Masters Cup in Shanghai.

Chapter quotes

Chapter One: taken from *The Swimmer* by Eleanor Perry

Chapter Two: taken from the *Palo Alto Weekly*, online edition, 27 September 2000

Chapter Three: reproduced with kind permission Universal Music Publishing

Chapter Four: taken from the *Sunday Telegraph*, 2 July 2000

Chapter Five: taken from *Sex & Drugs & Rock 'n' Roll: The Life of Ian Dury* by Richard Balls (Omnibus Press)

Chapter Six: taken from the sleevenotes to the album *Madness: The Business*, reproduced with kind permission from Suggs, Virgin Records and Rudge Management

Chapter Seven: *Observer Sport Monthly*, February 2002

Chapter Eight: *Daily Telegraph*, 27 December 1999

Chapter Nine: reproduced with kind permission www.nyrock.com

Chapter Ten: reproduced with kind permission the *Lonely Planet Guide to Britain*

Chapter Eleven: taken from CBS SportsLine.com

Chapter Twelve: taken from www.bbc.co.uk/radio1 with kind permission Rough Trade Management

Chapter Thirteen: taken from www.crystalclouds.co.uk

Chapter Fourteen: taken from www.vivaroxymusic.com

Chapter Fifteen: *Daily Telegraph*, 21 October 2002